Hearing children read

CAMPUS

Hearing children read

Robin Campbell

Routledge
London and New York

First published in 1988 by
Routledge
a division of Routledge, Chapman and Hall
11 New Fetter Lane, London EC4P 4EE

Published in the USA by
Routledge
a division of Routledge, Chapman and Hall, Inc.
29 West 35th Street, New York NY 10001

Typeset in 10/12pt Times Itek Graphix by
BookEns, Saffron Walden, Essex

Printed in Great Britain by Biddles Ltd, Guildford

British Library Cataloguing in Publication Data

Campbell, Robin, *1937–*
Hearing children read.
1. Children. Reading skills. Development
I. Title
428.4′3

ISBN 0-415-00912-X

Contents

Acknowledgements

This book is the outcome of many years engaged in the teaching and research of reading in the primary school. More specifically my higher degree researches at the Open University and London University have highlighted the interaction of hearing children read. I am grateful to Tony Pugh, Elizabeth Goodacre, and Hazel Francis who supervised this research and encouraged my thinking about the activity of hearing children read. The research was very much based on the realities of the classroom and I am very much indebted to the headteachers, teachers, and children who made the research possible. This book is both about them and for them. I have also benefited from the many discussions with fellow primary school teachers, including those who took part in the research and those who have attended various in-service courses with which I have been associated. Thanks are also due to Jim Johnson, who read and commented upon an early draft of this manuscript, and to Denise Hughes, who typed numerous transcripts as well as the initial typing of this book. Any defects which are still apparent in the text are, of course, my responsibility.

The author and publisher would like to thank the following for permission to reproduce copyright material in this book: Collins Educational, *One, Two, Three and Away* by S.K. McCullagh; Edward Arnold (Publishers) Ltd, *Racing to Read* by A.E. Tansley and R.H. Nicholls; Thomas Nelson and Sons Ltd, *Mckee Readers*; Schofield & Sims Ltd, *Through the Rainbow* by E.S. Bradburne. Every effort has been made to obtain permission to reproduce copyright material throughout this book, if any proper acknowledgement has not been made, or permission not received, we would invite any copyright holder to inform us of this oversight.

Introduction

Encouraging and facilitating the development of reading in young children involves parents and teachers in many activities. Reading to the young child from a selection of worthwhile books and eventually reading with the child are likely to be among those activities. In addition as confidence is gained the role as the reader will more frequently be taken over by the child. In such circumstances the adult will guide and support the reader. Thus the adult will listen to the reading, consider the mistakes or miscues that are produced, and provide some comment, perhaps, to help the reader with any difficulties. The parent or teacher will also want to talk about the book, on occasions, before or after the reading – or both. It is evident, therefore, that when an adult hears a child read a number of decisions will need to be made about the nature of the activity. This book seeks to explore the interaction and to provide some guidelines for teachers to consider in their practice. The guidelines which were developed from work carried out in classrooms may also help the parents who wish to reflect upon their role as they listen to their children reading.

Evidence exists to indicate that the activity of hearing a child read would appear to be a popular practice among teachers. The survey conducted for the Bullock Committee (DES 1975) clearly indicated the considerable amount of time that was being devoted to the activity by infant and junior school teachers. Subsequently King (1978) and Gray (1979) amongst others have noted, in observational studies of infant classrooms, the extent to which a teacher may hear children read. Indeed Gray suggested that for many infant school teachers this was regarded as the single most important component of 'good practice'. A NATE (1985) publication indicated the continuing interest in this activity among primary school teachers. Derived from the work

1

of Hewison and Tizard (1980) considerable interest now exists on the role of parents who might hear a child read at home. Hannon *et al* (1985) have shown how this interest has developed and the way in which some projects (e.g. Jackson and Hannon 1981) attempt to provide guidelines for parents in order to support them as they hear a child read. The Schools Council project Extending Beginning Reading (Southgate, Arnold, and Johnson 1981) also noted an emphasis upon listening to a child's oral reading among junior school teachers. The report from that project was critical of the way in which the activity was used by teachers. That criticism emphasized the need for a more sustained exploration of what actually occurs as a child reads to his teacher.

Extending Beginning Reading studied the junior classroom, of children aged 7 to 9+, using observations and interviews. However, the actual words that were spoken by the teacher as she listened to a child read were not made available. An exploration of the teacher utterances as she responds to the reader may provide illuminating insights into this teaching activity. Much of this book is therefore devoted to a consideration of the words spoken by a teacher as she hears a child read within a normal classroom setting. The examples in this book are of the teachers of infant children. Therefore, unlike the children in the Extending Beginning Reading project, the children are at an early stage of reading development. Even earlier examples of adults reading to children or various forms of shared or paired reading are not exemplified in this book. The emphasis here is on teachers hearing children read in infant schools as a stage towards independent and silent reading.

Most of the transcripts which are provided come from a study of infant school teachers who took part in a Hearing Children Read (HCR) project (e.g. Campbell 1981). Each teacher was observed at work in the classroom. Audio-recordings were made of the teacher as she heard children read during normal classroom lessons. The recordings were subsequently transcribed and formed the basis for an analysis of the interaction. The teachers were also interviewed in order to provide a dual perspective of the activity. This book is therefore about teachers at work in normal classrooms. The words of teachers and children are used wherever possible to indicate what was happening. It is hoped that the material which is presented will enable other teachers, and perhaps parents, to consider and analyse the detail of a common everyday teaching event for the benefit of their own work and the children they teach.

All the transcripts that are provided are presented in a format which indicates the reading from the book in the right hand column and the comments by the teacher, and less usually by the child, in the left hand column. Comments made by children other than the child reading have not been transcribed; indeed many of these comments were difficult if not impossible to decipher. However, any response by the teacher is indicated so that all the utterances by the teacher and the child reading during the interaction are provided. As an example of this format part of a transcript would appear as:

Darren		The children are having tea with the princess in the tower. They (There)
Teacher	Not they	
Darren		There are *silver* dishes on the table
Teacher	[aside] Yes, Julia, that's right.	
Darren	[reads on]	There are oranges and apples on the *silver* dish–dishes. I like having a **tea** party says the princess. I like /h/ /a/ – having a tea party. //Would you like to come into the castle? says the princess.

Key to the coding:

1	They (There)	:	word spoken and (word in text).
2	*silver*	:	word omitted by reader.
3	[aside]	:	comment by teacher to another child.
4	[reads on]	:	reads on without a pause.
5	dish–dishes	:	repetition or reconsideration of a word, including self-correction.
6	having a **tea** party	:	'tea' has been inserted by the reader.

3

| 7 | /h/ /a/ – having | : | reader is sounding out letters of the word. |
| 8 | //Would you like | : | reader hesitates before 'Would'. |

By presenting the transcript in this format it is possible to explore three main features of the interaction. The reading and miscues by the child can be noted; the teacher's response to the child reading as well as the teacher asides can be detected, and the outcome of the teacher guidance may be evident.

Thus in the brief example that is provided it can be noted that Darren miscued the text word (There) and uttered 'They'. The teacher responded to that miscue with her utterance 'Not They', which simply informed Darren of his miscue. The outcome of that intervention was that Darren corrected his miscue and carried on reading, albeit omitting the word 'silver'. That omission and the subsequent insertion of 'tea', both of which may have been indicative of Darren's actively processing the text and developing a flow to his reading, received no teacher response. The teacher would appear to have been more concerned with sharing the activity and encouraging meaningful reading rather than intervening after each miscue.

In subsequent chapters of this book a consideration of various aspects of the activity will be pursued. Thus in the first chapter the need for an appropriate classroom organization, to provide the opportunity for a teacher to hear a child read, is emphasized. One complete transcript and extracts from another interaction are provided. In the first example Brian reads to his teacher, she responds in a variety of ways to his miscues, and this interaction is analysed to indicate certain positive features of a teaching/learning experience. The second example has extracts from Neil reading to an inattentive and busy teacher; these extracts reaffirm the importance of classroom organization. The chapter ends with an indication of the overall structure of these teacher–pupil interactions. This, then, sets the scene for Chapters 3, 4, and 5.

Before dealing in some detail with the structure, however, Chapter 2 explores the purposes which provide the justification for the activity. What do teachers see as the purpose for hearing children read and how is this exemplified by actual teacher behaviour? Examples from transcripts are provided to clarify teacher views and theoretical statements.

In Chapter 3 the preliminaries to hearing a child read are explored.

Thus the physical aspects of the interaction, where the activity takes place; the organizational demands to reduce asides caused by attention switching and the length of the interaction are each considered. This then leads to an examination of the teacher–child exchanges which occur prior to the child beginning to read.

Once the child begins to read from the text miscues will be evident. How should the teacher respond to these miscues? Should all miscues receive some response from the teacher? Which teacher verbal moves may be most helpful to the reader? (A teacher verbal move may be part or all of the teacher utterance; each move serves a particular pedagogical function. Therefore a teacher who responds to a reader with 'No. What is the first sound?' has used two moves: first, a move of negative feedback and second, a move to emphasize the use of phonics.) These are the questions which are central to Chapter 4, 'Hearing a child read'. In this context it is evident that the notion of 'hearing' includes an active role for the teacher. She hears what the child reads, compares the reading with the text, diagnoses the appropriateness of the miscue, then responds or not based on that diagnosis. The teacher response as we shall see varies in its format and, therefore, the demand it places upon the child. However the teacher also needs to ensure that an appropriate social relationship is established within the activity. She will therefore need to consider how her actions and words will convey to the reader that a genuine collaborative activity is taking place.

Chapter 5 considers the completion of the interaction. Once the child has finished reading from the text, most usually a teacher decision, what questions will be asked of him? Various types of questions are explored; these include questions concerned with personal experiences, comprehension of words within the text and the text itself, word recognition, and phonics. The way in which the interaction is finally brought to a close is also explored.

A final chapter suggests guidelines for hearing a child read. These guidelines arise directly from the earlier chapters, especially the discussion of the transcripts. Throughout the book a substantial use is made of these transcripts. The utterances of the children and their teachers can and do provide useful insights into a commonplace interaction which until very recently had not received a close observation and analysis.

It will already have been noted that in order to avoid confusion within the text the teachers are referred to as she, and the child for general purposes as he. This is not meant to suggest any sexual discrimination. Perhaps more importantly it will also have been noted that the activity is referred to as hearing children read, although comment has been made, above, of the active role of the teacher and arguments have been provided elsewhere (e.g. Arnold 1982 and NATE 1985) that listening rather that hearing should more adequately describe the event. Within this book an emphasis upon the nature of the teacher participation will be evident. Hearing children read is used as a descriptor to reflect the term used by many classroom teachers. It is the nature of that activity rather than the title which may require attention.

Chapter one

A scene from an infant classroom

Inside the infant classroom the children are involved with various activities. One group of children are working with mathematical apparatus and recording their observations on paper. Some children are busy writing about their own world and experiences. Other children are 'playing' with sand or water. The water play involves using measuring jugs, cylinders, funnels, and plastic piping. Elsewhere in the classroom a model is being created out of cardboard boxes and tubes. A few children are at easels painting.

The teacher moves from group to group. Some children she encourages to explore other ideas. Others she praises, assists, or suggests future developments. Then, at an appropriate moment when all the activities appear to be running smoothly, she returns to her desk. When the teacher is seated at her desk she calls one of the children. Brian collects his book and stands beside the teacher with his book in front of them ready to read.

Teacher	What's Simon doing?
Brian	Jumping down the stairs, same as me.
Teacher	Do you jump down the stairs, or not?
Brian	Yes.
Teacher	Do you?
Brian	When I get out of bed I go yippee and jump down the stairs.
Teacher	Come on then.
Brian	Every day I get up and put on my clothes. I wash myself. I put on my white vest first.

Then my yellow shirt with the zip –
with a zip.
I do the zip up – I do *up* the zip
myself.

I don't get that.

I do *up* the zip myself.

Teacher   Well he does the zip up himself.

Brian

I look in the mirror and do my hair.
Then I go down stairs to have break-
fast.

I go down 10 stairs.

Teacher   Ah, ah.

Brian

I look in the mirror and do my hair.
Then I go down **the** – Then I go
down stairs

Teacher   That's right.

Brian

to have breakfast.
I go down 10 stairs.
If–If I am in a hurry I jump – I jump
down the stairs.
Mummy does not like me jump – to–
to jump
down–down the stairs.
She–she says,
Simon, you are naughty – not to
jump down the stairs.
You are to walk **down** – You are to
walk.
Then I walk down.
My first – My first (friend) My first
end Peter

Teacher   So who would it be?
My

Brian   My first end

Teacher   No.
Who is Peter to Simon?
His . . .

Brian   Friend.

My friend Peter and I

like to play on the stairs.
I (We) climb up to the top
and then we jump down – we jump
down.
We hide under the stairs
then–then–when we play hide and
seek.

Teacher	So what do they do on the stairs?
Brian	They jump down.
Teacher	And play don't they?
Brian	

I have breakfast with **my** mummy
and daddy
and Elizabeth.
I have breakfast with them every day.
My baby has breakfast with us too.
We have eggs and tea for breakfast.
I–I like brown eggs for my breakfast.
Then (When) I

Teacher	Ah, ah.
Brian	

Then–When I have finished breakfast
I go to school.
I go to school on a bus.
I go on the bus every–every school
day.
It is not fair–far to go–to go–to
school on a (the) bus.
I like to go on the top deck
and I like to be at the front,
then I like (can)

Teacher	then
Brian	

I can see out of the window.
I see my friend Peter on the bus.
He–He and has–He and his sister
came to–come on the bus
with Elizabeth and me.

Teacher	What does Simon have for his breakfast then?
Brian	Can you–I read this page?
Teacher	What does Simon have for his breakfast?
Brian	Eh.

Oh yes – brown eggs.

Teacher	Yes.
Brian	And tea.
Teacher	What do you have?
Brian	Cornflakes.
Teacher	You have cornflakes?
	Anything else?
	Emh.
Brian	Sometimes eggs, sometimes chips.
Teacher	Chips for breakfast.
Brian	Yes, chips, eggs, and bacon.
Teacher	For your breakfast, it sounds more like a dinner or a tea.
Brian	Can I read this page?
Teacher	Go on then last page for today.
Brian	This is my teacher.
	I like my teacher.
	I am /l/–learning to read to–at
	school.
	I read to my teacher every day.
	This is me reading to her.
	I have–I have read 20 books.
	I work every–I work every (very)
Teacher	No.
	I work
Brian	very had–hard at school.
Teacher	Well done Brian.
	That's lovely.
	Do you work hard at school?
Brian	Yes.
Teacher	Yes.
	Well done.

This interaction between the teacher and a child is typical of many such interactions which involve the teacher and a young reader reading from his current book. It is interesting to note how Brian appeared to be actively processing the text in order to gain meaning. He frequently produced repetitions and those repetitions or restarts seemed to be used to provide time to consider the text or to have a rerun at a word. Such a view is made apparent in the transcripts and emphasized by listening to the recordings of Brian as he read aloud. The teacher listened to the reader, compared his reading to that of the text, and on the basis of her view of reading and her knowledge of the child responded in a systematic manner. Later on the basis of her diagnosis on the way the child has read she may ask some questions to provide a short teaching interaction.

What are some of the noticeable features of the teacher interaction with Brian? The interaction was opened with an exchange, albeit briefly, about the text to be read. As in a conversation there was a gradual development to the main body of the interaction. When Brian began to read he omitted 'up' and later inserted 'the'. However the teacher did not perceive those as miscues which required immediate attention so she did not intervene. Brian continued to read and it was not until he miscued 'friend' and uttered 'first' and subsequently 'first end' that the teacher intervened and attempted to guide Brian towards the text word. Thus it would appear that the teacher did not intervene for all the miscues; she waited to give time for Brian to work it out for himself and she provided guidance to help him towards aspects of the text and the meaning where that was perceived to be necessary.

Following the reading of a few pages the teacher questioned Brian about the text and his own personal experiences. The interaction was being brought to an end by the teacher. However Brian demonstrated his view of the interaction as a shared activity by asking if he could continue by reading another page and the teacher agreed. Following that the teacher again made a few comments before finally she closed the interaction with a single question and some praise for Brian.

Hearing children read might then provide the opportunity for shared enjoyment, diagnosis, and teaching. The interaction between Brian and his teacher indicated that this can occur within the normal classroom setting. However, in order to have a genuine shared enjoyment of the text, the teacher needs to be sufficiently organized to ensure that the other children in the classroom are able to work on various activities while the interaction occurs. The importance of classroom organization has been stressed appropriately by Southgate, Arnold, and Johnson (1981) and Arnold (1982). Unless the teacher first attends to this fundamental part of her work then almost inevitably the hearing of a child read will not be successful. In the vast majority of interactions which were recorded in the HCR project the teacher was sufficiently organized to ensure that a worthwhile interaction occurred. However the following example only too vividly demonstrates the problems that can arise where the teacher is not sufficiently organized and therefore not ready to hear a child read.

Teacher   Neil reading please.
            [aside] Where's Keith?
            [aside] Oh, okay.
            [aside] How many pennies.
            [aside] Where?
            [aside] How many pennies, you tell me.
            [aside] There's not ten pennies there.
            This side Neil please.
            [aside] Go and do it again.
            [aside] Yes, it doesn't say that you see.
            [aside] It says how many pennies, count them. Right,
                draw them and count them.
            [aside] How many more do you need to make ten
                pennies.
            [aside] Go on.
            [aside] Draw those eight first, right.
            Page nineteen.

The beginning of this interaction clearly indicated that the teacher was not ready to hear Neil read. She was still very involved with other children. Consequently Neil received very little attention from his teacher and there was no notion of a shared activity in this opening of the interaction. Matters did not improve and as can be seen in a subsequent extract Neil was reading from the text with very little support from or involvement with his teacher.

Neil   She wants to come down.
                            Oh, White hen, said Dick.
                            We will come up and get you.
Teacher   Right.
Neil   Dick–Look Dick, said Jane.
Teacher   [aside] You've got six pennies, right. How many more
                do you need to make ten.
Neil   [reads on]   Oh (Do) you *see what I see*.
                            Is it the hen?
Teacher   [aside] One, two, three, four, five, six, right.
Neil   [reads on]   *Is it Spot?*
                            Is it Puff?

Teacher   [aside] Right one, two, three, four, five, six.
Neil   [reads on]   *No, said Dick.*
                        It is not a hen.

There is, perhaps, no need to examine those two extracts in detail. It would appear to have become no more than a ritualized activity in the classroom (Goodacre nd). No wonder the Extending Beginning Reading project was critical of such interactions. The teacher gave very little attention to Neil, who appreciated that point and during his reading began to omit large sections of the text. Why read out aloud if your audience is no longer listening? However, examples of this kind were rare in the Hearing Children Read project. In most instances the interaction provided a more positive teaching event (Campbell 1981). The teacher usually appeared to be involved in a shared activity with the child who was reading. Within that sharing the teacher often diagnosed and responded to the child's reading with what Morris (1974) referred to as on-the-spot treatment.

What, then, is the normal structure of hearing a child read? The earlier example of Brian reading to his teacher indicated that there is a preliminary exchange prior to reading; then a substantial part of the interaction is devoted to the child actually reading from his book and finally another exchange after the reading is completed. A normal pattern is illustrated in the diagram.

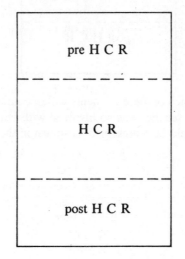

In the interaction between Brian and his teacher Brian actually returned to his reading after the teacher's first attempt to conclude the session. Therefore that interaction would more appropriately be represented in the second diagram.

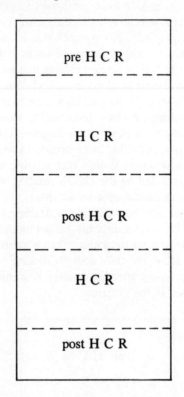

The length of each of these elements will of course vary. In Neil's case, because the teacher was so involved with other activities, the total structure would be represented as shown in the third diagram.

Of course, there may be occasions when this structure would be appropriate. However, in Neil's case the structure developed in that way for more negative reasons. As we shall see later (Chapters 3 and 5) there may be reasons why the teacher would adopt patterns more akin to the fourth and fifth diagrams.

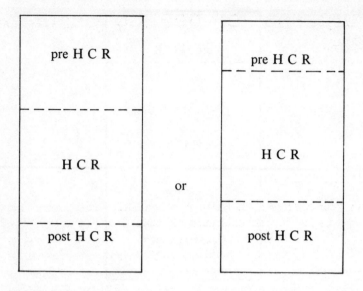

However, these patterns develop for positive instructional reasons arising from earlier diagnosis. Needless to say the length of the interaction will also vary according to the time available, the teacher's perception of the child's need, and the ability of the child to sustain his reading.

Before developing these ideas, it will be useful to provide a reminder of the purposes which provide the reasons for teachers hearing children read. The next chapter will consider that topic.

Chapter two

Purposes for hearing children read

Why hear children read? Helen Arnold (1982) has suggested that diagnostic and instructional purposes should provide the reasons. This is not dissimilar from the view that diagnostic and subsequent structuring of learning experiences partly provide the reasons for hearing children read (Atkinson and Gains 1973). Indeed Atkinson and Gains argued that this may be one of the most valuable reading activities for the teacher to work together with a young reader. Either the instruction can and does take place during the interaction and is therefore following an instant diagnosis and recognition of the child's needs, or it does, as Atkinson and Gains indicate, follow the interaction with a diagnosis leading to the development of subsequent learning experiences. There are, however, other purposes which may be regarded as important. These purposes, together with diagnosis and instruction, will therefore be considered. The purposes are derived from two sources. First, a group of teachers were questioned as to their purpose in hearing children read (Campbell 1982). The teachers were asked to indicate more than one purpose if they considered that to be appropriate. Second, there are those purposes which are stated in teachers' manuals for reading schemes or in general texts on the teaching of reading. The purposes which thus form the basis for discussion are:

1 to help children to learn to read;
2 develop interest and enjoyment;
3 reinforce personal relationships;
4 give the child practice of reading;
5 develop fluency and expression;
6 check and develop comprehension;
7 diagnosis;

8   check on progress;
9   check on accuracy;
10   instruction;
11   encouraging the use of contextual clues;
12   teaching phonics.

These purposes are clarified where appropriate with examples drawn from transcripts.

To help children to learn to read

Perhaps this purpose is so self-evident that it can be lost as teachers systematically provide a variety of reasons for hearing children read. And yet it must be the paramount reason for the teacher as she organizes her room in order to provide the opportunity to listen to a child reading. As Margaret Meek (1982) has so clearly argued, in order to learn to read the child requires the attention of a patient adult (or an older child) together with an interesting book, and this can form the basis for a genuine collaborative activity leading to success.

Within the infant classroom stories will be read to the children, writing will take place, in some cases a child will read together with the teacher (Waterland 1985) and many will have reached the point of reading to the teacher and receiving her sensitive support. Each of these might contribute to the child's development as a reader. Hearing children read can therefore be seen to provide a basis for helping children to learn to read. But it does require the teacher to think about the activity, to prepare for it, and to ensure that it remains a genuine collaborative event and does not become a ritual, as was noted in Chapter 1 when Neil read to his teacher.

Develop interest and enjoyment

A majority of teachers suggested in the HCR survey that the development of interest and enjoyment of reading was an important purpose for hearing children read. However, the difficulty of achieving that with books from some basic reading schemes was noted. The teachers argued that it can be difficult to promote an interest in the story if the content is trivial and the language stilted. However, it was recognized that these basic books do manage, especially some recent schemes, to provide adequate stories and language after the first few books.

Nevertheless, the question remains how does the interaction between the teacher and child actually provide an opportunity for developing an enjoyment of reading? A view put forward was that it is the actual sharing of an activity which is the contributory factor. Perhaps it is the attitude of the teacher which is crucial. As Kohl (1973) has suggested, it is difficult to teach that which you do not value. The children will soon assess their teachers' beliefs despite what the teachers might say themselves. If this is so, the manner in which the teacher approaches the interaction may be of considerable importance. If the teacher enjoys reading and can convey that message to the children in her class both by word and action, perhaps during the shared activity of hearing children read the child can be helped to share that enjoyment. A link might be drawn between this notion and the decisive factor influencing children's progress, as put forward by Southgate (1968), that is reading drive, the beliefs and attitudes of the teachers. What is clear from this discussion is the essential need to organize the classroom so that a meaningful interaction occurs. Again using the interaction in Chapter 1 between the teacher and Neil as an example, that was most unlikely to be fostering an enjoyment of reading. The need is for sensitive teaching (Butler and Clay 1979) which demonstrates a real involvement of the teacher with the child's reading.

Reinforce personal relationships

Amongst the teachers surveyed this was seen as an important purpose. As Goodacre (1976) has noted teachers do see the interaction as providing an opportunity to reinforce the personal relationships between teacher and child. The interaction is therefore seen to serve affective as well as cognitive purposes. Natchez (1975) and Clark (1976) have both argued that an interested adult, who demonstrates both an interest in the child's reading and a caring attitude about how things are going, may be instrumental in the child's progress with reading.

An intensive study of one teacher throughout a school year demonstrated the importance of providing a sensitive and accepting role while listening to a reader (Campbell 1986). That study demonstrated that where the child felt secure within the interaction he would interrupt his reading to talk about the text, indicate his knowledge or lack of knowledge about words and even enquire about

19

the teacher's health. In many respects this willingness of the child to stop and talk about the text is demonstrative of a genuine shared activity in which both members feel that they have the 'right' to digress and provide a comment. Under such conditions the interaction is not constrained by perceptions of the formal role of the teacher and the learner; rather a collaborative exercise is evident.

The interaction may also provide an opportunity to motivate the child to want to read and give him a sense of achievement. Roberts (1973) has argued that hearing children read provides the opportunity to satisfy the child's need for approval and backing. The report from West Sussex County Council (1976) emphasizes the relational aspect of the interaction to the extent of suggesting that this might involve physical contact as an expression of the confidence in the person to whom they are reading. For very young readers the child may want to sit on the teacher's lap (Waterland 1985) as an extension, perhaps, of reading experiences at home. However, older children in the infant classroom may want to sit or stand beside their teacher. Whatever is the case the physical contact may be an expression of the emotional link between the teacher and child. Each of the above views highlight the need for the teacher, when she hears a child read, to demonstrate her interest, to respond to the reader's needs, and remain as an audience for his reading. This provides an apposite reminder of the requirement to organize the classroom adequately so that these criteria can be met. The teacher will be able to relate to the reader only if her main attention can be with the reader. The other children in the classroom must be positively catered for by the prior organization of various activities in the room.

Give the child practice of reading

Stated quite simply, hearing children read provides the opportunity for the child to practise his reading. Behind this notion of the importance of providing the opportunities for children to practise their reading is the assumption that, although help with component skills may be of some assistance to the child, essentially what he requires to learn to read is to read. This might be linked to Frank Smith's central theme:

> to learn to read children need to read. The issue is as simple and difficult as that.
>
> (Smith 1978:5)

In more pragmatic terms what is perhaps being suggested is that the effective teacher of reading ensures that sufficient time is given to the activity of reading in order to assist the child's reading development (Harris 1979). Practice at reading, like practice at playing a piano, will ensure that the skill develops (Bissex 1980).

Of course, it can be argued that this practice might occur silently. The child could read to himself and the teacher's task would then be to ensure that adequate time is devoted to sustained silent reading. However, what might then be missing, especially during the early stages of reading, would be the presence of an information-providing adult (Smith and Goodman 1971). The child by reading aloud to his teacher does receive information as to how appropriate are his predictions of the reading. Practising his reading aloud to a teacher, with information and teaching provided in return, may be important for early reading development.

Develop fluency and expression

The development of fluency and expression was regarded as an important purpose by teachers in the HCR project. But how is this stated purpose achieved? A first approach might be by ensuring that the reading material is at the appropriate level for the child (Betts 1946) which would allow the child to read with rhythm, that is proper phrasing and accurate interpretation of punctuation. Or possibly by the teacher intervening to provide a model of reading for the child to attempt to imitate.

Lisa	He will not eat it, says the farmer.
	He does not like hay.
	When he is a big horse he will eat it.
Teacher	Now let's read it from here.
	And see if you can read it like this.
	Listen. I will do it gently.
	I will hold it out on my hand.
	He will not eat it, says the farmer.
	See if you can sort of make it go as though you were telling a story.
	Instead of saying When-he-is-a-big-horse.
	Try and put it all together.
	Start from here.
	I will do
Lisa	I will do it gently.

21

Lisa would appear, on this limited evidence, to be reading beyond a frustration level or an instructional level. She may already be reading at an independent level but nevertheless the teacher intervenes to provide a model of reading in an attempt to develop more fluency and expression.

There is little evidence to suggest that authors of books on the teaching of reading see this purpose as important, although Goodacre (1976) does indicate that she has previously noted that many teachers do place considerable emphasis on fluency in reading which includes use of pitch and expression, few mistakes, and no re-reading or back-tracking in the text. However, as Goodacre indicated, to eradicate the child's miscues is to deny the teacher evidence of the child's learning strategies. There is an apparent conflict here between on the one hand a wish to develop fluency and expression and on the other hand a wish to explore the child's miscues in order to ascertain strengths and weaknesses. This apparent conflict serves as a timely reminder that a teacher needs to consider each child individually and then determine the purpose for hearing him read. For some children fluency of reading might be appropriate at certain times, while at other times it might be more appropriate to assess their learning strategies by an analysis of miscues. The reading material would, therefore, need to be considered in relation to the purpose of the reading on any specific occasion.

Check and develop comprehension

Hearing children read as an opportunity for estimating the child's understanding of what he is reading has been suggested by Moyle (1968), Morris (1974), and Goodacre (1976). The Bullock Report developed that notion further and suggested that the teacher can ask questions to develop various kinds of comprehension, implying that comprehension questions may be asked at various levels and indeed at another point the report did put forward a taxonomy of comprehension skills (Barrett 1968). This is clearly seen as an important purpose when hearing children read and it was one of the most frequently stated purposes amongst teachers surveyed in the HCR project.

How is the level of comprehension to be assessed? The clearly stated view of the Bullock Report is by asking questions of the child. However, an alternative view might be that the teacher judges almost intuitively to what extent the child is reading with understanding.

Perhaps this intuition is based upon the flow of reading from the child, the extent to which he reads with expression, and also the degree to which any miscues are good miscues syntactically and semantically. An assessment of comprehension as the child reads may be based on the teacher's listening to this flow, expression, and estimate of miscue appropriateness. However, at other times she does quite clearly ask questions in order to test that the child has extracted meaning from the text. These questions may occur before the reading begins. They may relate to illustrations or to parts of the text already read on a previous occasion. The questions set the scene for what is about to be read.

Teacher	Come on then, Rachel.
	Right Rachel wait a moment.
	Let's have this over here.
	Rainbow's End.
	What was this story about?
	'Cos you're half way through it aren't you.
Rachel	Broken down van.
Teacher	Broken down.
	Was it a broken down van or a broken down lorry?
Rachel	Broken down lorry.
Teacher	Broken down lorry.
	How did it break down?
Rachel	Oh.
Teacher	You don't know.
Rachel	I can't remember now.
Teacher	You can't remember.
	Well you think about it, look.
	Where were the children going anyhow?
Rachel	They were going to have a picnic.
Teacher	They were going to have a picnic.

More frequently the questions occur after the child has read the text. The questions may check on the reader's general understanding of the text.

Simon	The tree shook and there was a crack as the—as it came crashing to the ground.
	Randy was happy.
	At last he had pulled down a tree

and now he knew that he was
growing strong.

Teacher	Beautifully read.
	Well done Simon.
	How was Randy pulling down the tree?
	With his hands?
Simon	His trunk.

However the teacher may also explore specific word meanings.

John	across the road and
	there were three planks over it.
	Roger put his foot on the middle
	plank.
	The plank tipped up.
Teacher	What's a plank?
John	It's a piece of wood.

She may also relate that text to the child's own experience. This is evident in the example above as the interaction continued, although in this case the questioning is at a somewhat superficial level.

Teacher	Yes.
	Have you ever played on a plank?
John	Yes.
Teacher	Yes.
	It's like a see-saw isn't it if you put it on the right part.

Rather than accepting the simple 'yes' reply the teacher might have used an enabling strategy (Tough 1979) in order to encourage John to a fuller response which would have more adequately indicated his experience. Thus she could have asked, 'So what did you do?', given time for him to respond, and perhaps if required sustained John in his thinking and response with simple encouragers such as 'mm'.

Diagnosis

Joyce Morris (1974) has indicated her view of the importance of hearing children read in order to diagnose the child's reading strengths and weaknesses.

It is taken as understood that teachers will
carry out this necessary activity [hearing children read]
for diagnostic-teaching purposes.

(Morris 1974: 35)

This quotation neatly encapsulates the widely held view that hearing children read is an activity which enables teachers to diagnose the difficulties the child may be encountering. Dean (1968), Moyle (1968), Hughes (1970; 1972; 1973), Ireland (1976), and Goodacre (1976) all emphasized the diagnostic purpose when hearing children read. Also Vincent and Cresswell (1976) were perhaps suggesting the possibilities of hearing children read being a diagnostic activity when they stressed the importance of the experienced and skilled teacher in reading as the best diagnostic testing device. Mackay, Thompson, and Schaub (1970) stressed that there is an implication that more diagnostic records should be developed from such activities, while Herber (1966) argued that such diagnosis provides the opportunity for testing and teaching to be integrated, thus allowing for what Morris (1974) referred to as on-the-spot treatment. The diagnosis is carried out in order to provide appropriate subsequent instruction.

In the American literature the diagnosis of oral reading, possibly by miscue analysis, is well documented. However, Dolch (1961) argued the case for diagnosis not just in clinics but by the many teachers who deal every day with children. In this country Potts (1976), although arguing a case against the activity of hearing children read, did suggest that if the activity occurred, it must be for diagnostic purposes.

The Bullock Committee argued that hearing children read should be seen as a major diagnostic opportunity for the teacher, although its members noted that at that time the diagnostic possibilities were largely unrealized. Although this may have been the case, Goodacre (1976) suggested that, based upon personal impression, teachers were adopting a more diagnostic approach to teaching reading especially related to the more active listening to chidren's reading aloud and their miscues/errors.

The teachers who were studied in the Hearing Children Read project suggested that an important purpose was 'to diagnose difficulties'. However there was also recognition that this in itself was insufficient and the purpose might be regarded as 'to observe child's difficulties and to treat them'. The diagnosis leads to instruction. A dominant feature of the interactions which were observed was that diagnosis leads to instruction. Frequently that instruction was the on-the-spot treatment of a miscue as the child read from his text.

Andrew	Jennifer stood by the gate,
	looking at the little black horse.
	She called (could) see
Teacher	She
Andrew	She could–could see he was not very old.

Andrew's reading of 'could' was miscued – he said 'called'. The teacher's diagnosis was that this altered the meaning so she provided instruction. This was quite simply to restart the sentence, a word cueing strategy, and Andrew then read on. The various strategies that the teacher uses will be considered in Chapter 4. However, not only do teachers teach while listening to the reader but also they use that diagnosis to develop instruction after the reading is completed.

Ben	Would you like the–like to have it.
	Would I like–you like
	to play with it.
	Can you–Can you draw the picture– the train.
	What else can–What else work–What else would you like
	in the toy shop.
Teacher	Well would you like to have a train like that?
	Mm?
	And what is it made of?
Ben	Wood and clay.
Teacher	That's right.
Ben	No.
Teacher	No, but you were right.
	It's made of?
Ben	Wood.
Teacher	Wood.
	That's the wood the train is made of.
	But that's how you write–would you like to have it?

	There's two woods/woulds aren't there spelt differently?
	So that's would you like to have it.
	And would you?
Ben	Yes.
Teacher	Yes you would.
	Right well done Ben.
Ben	Bet you it's expensive.
Teacher	I bet you it is expensive.
	Yes.
	Well done, Ben.

Thus in this example it can be seen that as Ben finished his reading to the teacher for that day she used her diagnosis of his reading and of the text to ask about the text and Ben's preferences. She also followed Ben's self-correction sequence of 'can-work-would' to draw his attention to the similar sound and dissimilar appearance of wood/would. Thus the ending of the interaction was, at least in part, determined by the earlier diagnosis.

Check on progress

What might be meant by the simple statement of a purpose to check on progress? At least two interpretations are available. First, the check on progress might be suggesting the qualitative assessment of a child's developmental progress in reading. This would return us to the ideas of diagnosis based, perhaps, on miscue analysis leading to appropriate instruction. However, the purpose of checking on progress may be linked to a second far more limited view of keeping a check on the books and pages read in order to note the progress through a reading scheme. The rather limited records which are kept on children's reading (DES 1975) might suggest it is this second check on progress which occurs in many classrooms. However, it is obviously the first view of checking on progress as a qualitative assessment of reading which must be regarded as appropriate.

Check on accuracy

This purpose might suggest that the teachers who were questioned viewed reading as a precise process involving 'exact, detailed, sequential perception and identification of letters, words, spelling patterns and larger language units', as Kenneth Goodman (1967) put it; rather than his view of reading as a selective process in which tentative decisions are made, based on the use of available language cues, these decisions being subsequently confirmed, rejected, or refined as reading progresses.

If a teacher is checking on accuracy and then attempting to ensure that the reading is accurate, precision is being sought. However, this may not always be appropriate. First, there is a need to examine the miscue in relation to the text word. If the meaning is retained (for example 'There is a picture of the (a) tiger at the front of my book'), is exact reading of the word required? Perhaps this is very much dependent not only on the teachers view of the reading process but also on her view of the reader and his level of development. As a guide, however, Clay (1979), using McNaughton's ideas, suggested that if more than one miscue in ten is occurring, those miscues which hardly alter the meaning are unlikely to require attention.

The miscues which might receive attention and the way in which the teacher might best respond to the miscues is dealt with in some detail within Chapter 4.

Instruction

Hearing children read for purposes of instruction is, as we have already seen, the logical corollary to the earlier stated purpose of diagnosis. A teacher makes a diagnosis of the child's reading then either responds with immediate teaching or utilizes the diagnosis for subsequent structuring of learning experiences. As one of the teachers indicated, hearing a child read will 'help me to decide upon further activities he may require'.

The importance of developing subsequent teaching based upon earlier diagnosis has been stressed by Moyle (1968), Hughes (1972), and Morris (1974). Hearing children read enables the teacher to provide individual teaching matched to the child's perceived needs (Dean 1976). There is a demand, therefore, for the more qualitative observations while listening to children read leading to appropriate learning experiences (DES 1975).

A few examples of how this might happen have already been provided. A more detailed analysis of the teaching following on from hearing a child read is provided in Chapter 5.

Encouraging the use of contextual cues

Although this purpose was not articulated by more than a few teachers it is nevertheless implicit in a major, but simple, teaching strategy. When the reader miscues a word the teacher may quite simply restart the sentence and read up the miscued word. She does this with a rising intonation to indicate that a question is being asked, 'What is the next word?'

Nigel	Sun Dew may be looking for–for
	seeds.
	She may here (have)
Teacher	She may
Nigel	have gone to the /l/–ake–lake.

This word cueing strategy may encourage the use of contextual cues (both syntactic cues – how the sentence is constructed – and semantic cues – the meaning involved in the sentence). Although in the example above only the first two words of the sentence can be provided it does indicate how the syntactic and semantic information as well as the graphophonic (the features of the letters and associated sounds) (Goodman 1969) are again made available to Nigel. He is able to read the word. As will be noted later, this strategy often appeared to help the reader successfully continue with his reading. It is interesting to note that this is similar to the strategy of Helen, an able reader, in a study by Clay (1979). When she recognized her own miscue, Helen would frequently restart the sentence and this often enabled her to read the word.

Teaching phonics

One of the ways in which instruction occurs is through the teaching of phonics, or at least bringing the child's attention to letters and their associated sounds. The teacher may provide teaching within the time spent reading from the text and/or use the opportunity after the read to consider letters and sounds of words read. The teacher is therefore providing a teaching of phonics based upon the child's reading. This incidental or functional phonics teaching (Schonell 1951) was sup-ported by a substantial proportion of teachers surveyed for the

Bullock Report as well as in the Hearing Children Read project. A further example of how this incidental phonics teaching occurred is provided below.

Ian	Can you buy tea at your shop? Buy a packet of tea //
Teacher	What's this sound?
Ian	/f/
Teacher	/fr/
Ian	from the shop. Weigh the tea (packet).
Teacher	No, steady. Weigh the
Ian	packet of tea. You can // take the tea to the playhouse. You can have a tea party for the dolls. You can have the //
Teacher	/ch/ You can have the /ch/
Ian	chair (children)
Teacher	/chil/
Ian	children to tea.

Although in both instances the teacher's first attempt to get Ian to read the word through a reference to phonics does not achieve success, her subsequent development of the phonic teaching does enable Ian to read each of the words.

The incidental teaching of phonics covered a number of different strategies used by the teacher, she may:

1 Provide a general prompt: 'What's this sound?'
2 Provide a specific prompt: 'Look at the first letter(s).'
3 Provide phonic information: '/ch/'.
4 Remind the child of a so-called phonic 'rule': 'Now remember what the y gives at the end.'

5   Develop an appropriate word list after hearing the child read in order to stress a particular aspect of phonics.

All these strategies were noted in the observations and recordings of teachers Hearing Children Read.

However, there are a substantial number of teachers who would argue, as Frank Smith (1971) did, that phonics and phonic rules should not be taught, although children will increasingly learn about phonics as they interact with the text and receive support and guidance from their teacher. Furthermore, to have as a purpose 'teaching phonics' might be to conflict with purposes related to meaning, fluency, interest, and enjoyment. And as we shall note later in Chapter 4 teaching phonics during the course of an interaction often served to distract readers rather than helping them to continue reading the text. Therefore this aspect does need to be given very careful consideration before becoming part of the teacher's purpose when hearing a child read.

The purposes for hearing children read which have been put forward include:

1   to help children to learn to read;
2   develop interest and enjoyment;
3   reinforce personal relationships;
4   give the child practice of reading;
5   develop fluency and expression;
6   check and develop comprehension;
7   diagnosis;
8   check on progress;
9   check on accuracy;
10 instruction;
11 encouraging the use of contextual cues;
12 teaching phonics.

The teacher will need to decide how many of these purposes are applicable to a specific situation. Which purpose or purposes are particularly important with each child as he reads? The teacher must also consider in detail what this purpose means in actual teacher behaviour? How can the purposes be best achieved? The subsequent chapters will concentrate on actual teacher behaviour during hearing children read interactions.

Chapter three

Preliminaries to the child reading

It is assumed in this book that the teacher is hearing a child read within the setting of the normal classroom. Therefore, before the teacher can begin to be involved in listening to a young reader she must first organize her classroom adequately so that the children are involved in purposeful activities and are aware where help, or other activities, can be obtained without interrupting the teacher.

In Chapter 1 a brief description was provided of an infant classroom where the teacher adequately provided for the class before hearing Brian read. As it is after all the quality of the interaction which is of importance (Morris 1966), this prior organization is crucial in order that the teacher and child can enjoy a period of sustained interaction. This is, of course, very much part of the argument of the Extending Beginning Reading project (Southgate, Arnold, and Johnson 1981).

The book to be read by the child entails a major decision by the child and teacher. The Bullock Report (DES 1975) indicated the very considerable reliance that is placed, by teachers, upon the graded reading scheme. This has since been confirmed by a survey of primary school practice in England carried out by HM Inspectors of Schools (DES 1978). The use of such books is not without its critics, however, and Thackray (1980; 1981) provided details of the argument. The use of a more individualized reading programme has been suggested as a possible alternative to the graded reading scheme (Moon 1973). The real need may be for reading material that is both interesting and makes sense to the learner, as argued by Smith (1978) and Meek (1982). Various texts whether from graded schemes or not may serve such a purpose. Nevertheless whatever is the case the teacher must consider the important details of classroom organization and the book to be read before preparing to hear a child read. Although the crucial importance of the book to be read is not in doubt it is the nature of the interaction which is central to this text and we shall therefore turn our attention to that activity. What precedes the reading from the book?

The positioning of teacher and child

Given that we are considering a teacher in a normal classroom setting with thirty or more children to care for then an initial decision for the teacher must be concerned with details of where the interaction is to take place and the position of teacher and child. What are the possibilities? The teacher might move around the room and hear a child read at the desk or table where he is working. Alternatively she might utilize the library corner of the classroom as the focal point for the activity. In such cases the child might sit side by side with his teacher and at the same level, as suggested by Dan Tavener in the NATE (1985) collection of papers. Or younger infants could sit on the teacher's lap, as Waterland (1985) argued. However, the invariable choice of the teachers observed in the HCR project was to hear each child reading at the teacher's desk. One teacher did recall that this was contrary to advice received during initial training; nevertheless she heard children read at her desk.

Why should the activity have occurred at the teacher's desk. The crucial factor may have been that it allowed the teachers to remain in contact with and control of their class. She is able to display the 'withitness', demonstrating that she knows what is happening in the classroom, which Kounin (1970) argued was a key factor in classroom management. She will also be able to attend to more than one issue simultaneously, overlapping, to use Kounin's terminology, which again leads to successful classroom management. The teacher by positioning herself at her desk is able to see the class and react to any event that requires her attention. She can call individual children to her desk to read and the children, aware of the organizational structures in the room, readily respond to this request. An interesting feature of this aspect is the way in which the children readily appreciate the intonation patterns associated with the teacher's name calling.

Susannah   Andy came along the pavement
                                                                      again.

		He had on his circus clothes,
		and he had on new black shoes.
		You can–can't walk around the circus
Teacher	[aside] Matthew!	
Susannah	[reads on]	in those new shoes, Dot said.
		You had better // stop and take time
		to get shoes
Teacher	[aside] Helen.	
Susannah	[reads on] you can walk in.	

While Susannah was reading the teacher called two names, Matthew and Helen. However, there was no confusion as to the purpose of these two calls. Matthew altered his behaviour and returned to the task in hand, while Helen got her book and went to the teacher's desk to read. Another important feature of simply calling the child's name, and with intonation indicating the purpose of the call, is that there is minimal interruption to the child who might be reading at that moment.

Reading side by side

When the child arrives at the desk to read he stands beside his teacher who is sitting. This usually ensures that teacher and child are working at the same level, an aspect which Taverner (NATE 1985) also suggested was important. The reading takes place side by side rather than face to face (Veatch 1978). Not only does this clear the path of vision to the rest of the class but also, as Veatch argued, it may be better psychologically to work side by side which establishes the feeling of unity, of working together, with the book in front of them. Face to face might imply in opposition to one another. Working side by side does, then, provide the togetherness, the emotional link which provides the relevant educational setting for the activity to proceed.

The children are aware that they go to one particular side of the teacher's desk to read. Other children requiring assistance from the teacher are aware that they should always, at least while another child is reading to the teacher, go to the other side of the desk. (However, it is hoped that such requests would be minimized by the prior organization of the classroom.) The side-by-side reading is illustrated in the diagram.

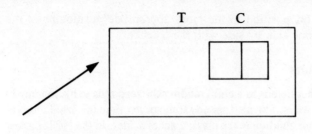

Key: Large rectangle represents teacher's desk
     T – Teacher
     C – Child

[|]   – Book position

➤ – Other children coming to the teacher for assistance

Although this pattern of reading side by side was true for the majority of interactions observed in the HCR project, there were occasions where variations were noted. For instance, Sean read initially with his book to his side (a) before moving beside the teacher and reading with his book in front of him (b).

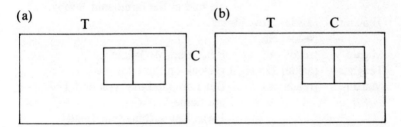

In this instance, as on other similar occasions, there was no discernible change in the quality or quantity of miscues! Yetta Goodman (1967) has made a similar observation with her study of six beginning readers, noting on one occasion that a reader turned his book completely upside down and continued reading without an overt pause. This is not to suggest that children should be encouraged towards such flexibility! As in Sean's case, noted above, and in all the HCR project observations where variations occurred, the child reading gradually rearranged his position to the more appropriate positioning of the child and book side by side with the teacher.

Teacher asides

As the teacher listens to a child reading she responds to his reading in a variety of ways. She also spends some of her time in verbal interaction with other children in the class: teacher asides. In the HCR project a mean of 12.8 asides per interaction was noted. However, this hides a wide variation in the use of asides, from interactions with no asides to those like Neil (Chapter 1), where a total of twenty-six asides did have a fundamental effect upon the activity. This switching of attention from the child reading to others in the classroom is, of course, not unique to the HCR project; it has been reported elsewhere (King 1978; Gray 1979; Southgate, Arnold, and Johnson 1981).

These asides are used for two main purposes. First, there are asides to direct, control, and organize the other children in the classroom: they are teacher-initiated moves. Second, there are asides which are a response to a child-initiated move, most usually involving a child coming to the teacher's desk to seek assistance.

Martin		Fun with Father.
		Oh, Father! What a good time
		we had at the farm! said Bobby.
Teacher	[aside] Now Simon.	
	[aside] Sh!	
Martin	[reads on]	Fine, said Mr White.
Teacher	[aside] Do eight o'clock on there for me.	
Martin	[reads on]	But I am glad that you and Ted
		are home.
		I was just wishing that I had
		someone to go fishing with me.

Examples of both types of asides are evident above. The teacher directed Simon by a move which indicated that she was aware that he was not doing what was expected of him. The second aside was a more general 'Sh!' to control the noise level in the class. The third aside was directed at a child who was at the teacher's desk with his mathematics book. These asides do not appear to disturb Martin in his reading of the text as he does not miscue. However, it is not possible to detect how much attention the teacher was paying to Martin's vocalization. Furthermore, it must be asked what effect such asides would have on Martin's perception of this as a shared activity! Why read to the teacher if she does not appear to be listening?

In another example Susannah miscued by hesitating before the word 'again'. Although the teacher was involved in an aside with Michael she was apparently still listening to Susannah as she immediately responded to the miscue. This might suggest that even though the teacher may be switching her attention between the reader and others in the classroom she might nevertheless remain in contact with the child who was reading.

Teacher	[aside] Michael!
Susannah	Andy came along the pavement//
Teacher	[aside] Well you have in the box where Michael is.
	again.
Susannah	again.
	He had on his circus clothes,
	and he had on//
Teacher	What does it begin with?

However, at times a child did miscue and because the teacher's attention may have been elsewhere the child did not receive the support that might have been required.

Michelle	Stop//
Teacher	[aside] Right so what's a quarter of eight?
Michelle	Stop//
Teacher	[aside] What would half be?
	[aside] What would half of eight be?
	[aside] Get a frame.
	Stop
Michelle	Stop//
Teacher	[aside] Four p.
	[aside] So what would a quarter be?
Michelle	Stop bus (here)
Teacher	Stop /h/
Michelle	here, said Mrs Red Hat.

Michelle hesitates in front of the word 'here'. It might be argued that she read the word 'Stop' three times as a means of leading into reading the word 'here'. However, she may also have been seeking quite simply to regain the teacher's attention and receive some instructional support. This example and the extracts with Neil noted earlier do serve to emphasize the importance of minimizing the number of asides by ensuring that the classroom is adequately organized to allow time for the teacher to hear a child read. However, no matter how well the classroom is organized the teacher will still have interruptions, either teacher or child initiated, to the activity, and Resnick (1972) argued that the teacher will have to respond to those interruptions from time to time in order to maintain an adequate degree of contact with all the children in the class.

Even though examples have been given to indicate that the teacher can switch her attention and still remain in contact with the reader, nevertheless it is important that the teacher attempts to minimize the asides. Her main attention needs to be centred upon the child and his reading performance. The careful prior organization of the classroom should permit that to occur.

Time spent hearing a child read

In the HCR project a mean of 4 minutes 36 seconds was noted during a period of 156 observations with 6 teachers. This indicated a substantially longer period of time being devoted to the interaction than was indicated by Southgate, Arnold, and Johnson (1981), with teachers of first and second year juniors, or Gray (1979), with infant school teachers. The even lower average, noted by King (1978) with infant school teachers, of 73 seconds was not matched by a single interaction in the HCR project, although there was one which at 78 seconds was close to the King average. However, at the other end of the range there was an interaction which lasted for 14 minutes 40 seconds.

Although the amount of time spent on the interactions is of some importance, especially perhaps to the overall classroom organization, it is the quality of the interaction which may determine the pedagogical value of such events (Morris 1966). For instance the 78-second interaction was shorter in length than either Boydell (1975) or Goddard (1958) would consider adequate for diagnostic and teaching purposes. However, closer perusal of that interaction might suggest otherwise.

Teacher	Right Helen.
	Where are we up to?
	Fifteen aren't we, Helen.
	[aside] What's the matter, Lisa?
	[aside] Bicycle, right.
	Right Helen.
Helen	Get into your trucks and follow me,
	said the big red tractor.
	I have helped
Teacher	[aside] Do the others?
Helen	[reads on] the chief of police and
	the fire chief.
	I got the mail from the post office
	to the railway station.
	I helped get the telephone lines up.
	Now I'm going to help you.
	Come on! It won't take long
	to get–to get these (those) water
	pipes working.
	And off went Katy
Teacher	[aside] Sandra.
Helen	followed by the men
	and the trucks from the water works.
	She took them to the people who had
	trouble with pipes–with water pipes.
Teacher	Very nicely read.
	Em, Katy went to get the mail didn't she?
	What is the mail?
	Can you tell me?
Helen	Letters and parcels.
Teacher	Good girl, letters and parcels.
	That's right.
	Good girl.
	Right.
	Off you go.

In this interaction there were opening verbal moves which suggest a collaborative exercise by the use of the pronoun 'we'. Helen, an able reader, read competently through one page of her book self-correcting an omission and substituting one word without loss of meaning. As

Helen completed the page she received positive feedback then was asked a comprehension question related to a word in the text. The interaction was closed with positive feedback and a clear indication of the interaction being terminated. Although a very clear case could be made for an extension of that interaction in order to allow for further diagnosis, instruction and a more detailed questioning of comprehension, nevertheless the activity did appear to constitute a teaching event with some positive aspects. The teacher was able to check on progress, make a limited diagnosis of the child's reading, and on the basis of that diagnosis ask a question to determine an understanding of word meaning. In contrast to that short interaction providing some positive features it can be noted that a long interaction may involve minimum contact between the child and the teacher. In an extract from Paul's reading it can be seen that he read alongside the teacher who was interacting with other children in the class.

Paul		That is old Mr Crow, said a duck.
		He is over there by the barn.
Teacher	[aside]	You'll have to do some writing practice.
Paul	[reads on]	The ducks, the hens, the chickens and
		the rooster ran across to the barn.
		There sat Mr Crow on the fence.
		What did you–What is it? they//
		they asked
Teacher		him.
	[aside]	Do those then I'll give you a word for each
		letter.
Paul		What is what?–What is what? asked
		the crow.
		Why did you call us? asked a–asked
		a hen.
		I didn't–I didn't,

That interaction which continued in a similar manner lasted for 6 minutes 12 seconds, almost 2 minutes longer than the mean. It did, however, contain twenty-nine teacher asides and it must be questioned as to whether the interaction was merely part of a ritual rather than a meaningful teaching event. However, it is not the purpose of this section to raise a polemic against long interactions. An extract from Mark's reading in the longest recorded interaction of the project,

14 minutes 40 seconds, demonstrated that these long interactions can, of course, contain more positive teaching events.

Mark	I would like to see the horses–horses first
	said–says
Teacher	No.
	You've missed a line.
Mark	Yes you can see the horses it – if you like,
	said (says) the farmer.
Teacher	Not said.
Mark	says the farmer.
	They are all out in the /f/ fens (fields)
Teacher	No.
	Where are they?
Mark	fields.
Teacher	That's right.
	Field.
	Is it field or fields?
Mark	fields.
Teacher	What makes it say fields?
Mark	It's got a /s/ at the end.
Teacher	That's right.
Mark	'Cos if it didn't have /s/ it would be field.
Teacher	Field that's right.
	They're out in the fields today.
Mark	Do
Teacher	Read that line again.
	Because you've lost track.
	This line here.
	They are
Mark	They are all out in the /f/
Teacher	That word!
Mark	fields today.

Mark made a number of miscues which the teacher attempted to repair by the use of various verbal moves. She also questioned Mark about his understanding of a plural ending. Within this example of hearing children read there was then some evidence of a meaningful discourse between the teacher and Mark. Although, based on that small extract, questions could be raised as to whether Mark was given sufficient opportunity to read the text, rather than responding as he did to questions about it.

Clearly, although the element of time is of some concern, it is the qualitative aspects of interactions which are of most importance (Boydell 1978). The mean in the HCR project of 4 minutes 36 seconds does provide a guide to an apropriate length for hearing a child read. A time of approximately 5 minutes has been similarly proposed by Veatch (1978) in America for the individual conference. Although there may be arguments put forward to lengthen the interaction to meet specific needs (and for junior classrooms this may be the case, as Vera Southgate argues: Southgate, Arnold, and Johnson 1981), nevertheless the outcome of such lengthening is to reduce the time available for other interactions. If the teacher is to develop relationships, observe, diagnose, teach, and record then a period of time close to 5 minutes may be required, but it will be the way in which she responds to the child as he reads which is of most importance.

Opening the interaction

It has already been noted how the teacher might call the child to read. However if a stated purpose of the interaction is to reinforce the one-to-one relationship, then it would seem appropriate that the interaction is subsequently opened with a teacher welfare move which attempts to meet this purpose and demonstrate the empathy of the teacher for the child.

Teacher	Now then Yolande we've had a little rest haven't we eh?
Yolande	Yes.
Teacher	Right let's see how much you've remembered eh?
Yolande	Mummy (Mother) and Daddy come (came) in.
Teacher	Good.

The teacher opened with a welfare move which not only served as a greeting but also indicated to Yolande the teacher's awareness of her absence from school. Possibly the remark hints that the teacher is aware that Yolande may find the reading difficult. Following Yolande's affirmation the teacher directed Yolande to read but again hinted that not every word might be remembered. Yolande's reading of the first line in the text included two miscues, a dialect variation, 'mummy'– 'mother', and a verb tense/dialect variation, 'come'–'came'. Despite this the teacher provided positive feedback. Although it is only the opening remark by the teacher which might be regarded as a welfare move, nevertheless it is possible to detect throughout the opening moves a general empathy for the child and a warm receptive start to the interaction. A similar use of welfare moves to open an interaction is demonstrated in another example.

Teacher	Now, John, you were away yesterday.
	Remember what the book was about?
	Because you had a holiday the day before didn't you?
	So you haven't read the book for about four days
	have you?
	What was your book called?
John	The Village (Billy)
Teacher	No.
	Billy and Percy
	It's a hard word that isn't it.

The opening remark by the teacher combined both welfare and comprehension moves. However, once John begins to read, the miscue of 'Village' for 'Billy' is such that the teacher provided negative feedback. She did in her next utterance, however, provide a further welfare move to indicate her empathy with the reader. Welfare moves will therefore appear within the interaction as well as opening the activity. Within the interaction those moves serve to emphasize the relationship between the teacher and the child indicating the concern of the teacher for the child. Often this may take the form of an apology following some form of interruption.

Mark	It was cold.
	And there was Willie
	out in the cold.
	Willie was a little kitten.
	He did not//know where–where to go.
Teacher	[aside] I think you had better come out now and do
	something else.

> Hold on a minute please Mark.
> [aside] Keith!
> [aside] Come out of the bricks.
> [aside] Out.
> [aside] Find something else to do on the shelf.
> Right.
> Sorry.

Additionally there were instances where a teacher followed up the conversation initiated by the child who was reading. The frequency of this type of move was perhaps related to the child's perception of the conversational rights within the interaction. Angela Hale (1980) suggested that, at least in junior classrooms, children would not initiate an exchange during the time that they were reading, However, among the children observed in infant classrooms in the HCR project, it was noted that they did feel that they could play a leading role in the conversation/interaction. Therefore examples of the children initiating an exchange could be noted (Campbell 1986) as could the teacher response with moves which demonstrated a willingness to accept the child's feelings and initiations.

Paul	My house has a red roof.
	It is a red roof.
Teacher	Mmh.
Paul	We've got a brown one haven't we?
Teacher	What on your house?
Paul	Mm.
Teacher	You've got a brown roof on your house have you?
	I think my roof on my house is a black one.

In addition, as might be expected, welfare moves often concluded the interaction, as we shall see in Chapter 5. However, this section has been concerned with the opening of the interaction. It is important, for affective reasons, that the child feels he is being welcomed to the activity. The scene is therefore set for an instructional interaction with an element of personal warmth.

Questions prior to the reading

Although on occasions the teacher may wish to proceed directly to hearing the child read after the opening welcome, as with Yolande above, at other times she might consider it appropriate to bring the child's attention to a previous read. This might take the format of making reference to problems which were diagnosed by the teacher and which were recorded for subsequent teaching.

Teacher	What does that begin with?
	Try to match up the blue word with the blue word.
Colin	thank (track).
Teacher	No, no, no.
	What does it begin with?
	First letter.
	Mm.
Colin	tank (track).
Teacher	No.
Colin	trank (track).
Teacher	/tr/
	Sound it.
Colin	/tr/ /a/ /ck/ track, back, sack.
Teacher	Good boy.
	Right.

Or, as in another example:

Teacher	Did you read a page to your Mum?
Alan	Two.
Teacher	Two.
	That was good.
	Now Alan.
Alan	I know – I know what this word says: wash.
Teacher	Wash.
	Good lad.
	What about this word, though?
Alan	Have.
Teacher	Good lad.
	I can cross that word off your list.

In the first of these examples the teacher is emphasizing the word ending '–ack' and in the second example words which had been miscued in context were examined out of context. Alan managed to read both the words from a list on his reading card. An interesting additional feature of the interaction with Alan is the reference to his mother. This encouragement of reading at home as well as in school may add substantially to reading development (Hewison and Tizard 1980) and attempts to increase the links between home and school are increasingly evident.

The pre-reading part of the interaction might also more frequently take the form of the teacher asking a number of comprehension questions which range from simple recall, 'What's the name of the two children in the story?', to questions which in appearance make demands of inference, 'How do you know they have only been once?' There were also questions which related the story content to the child's own experience, 'Have you been on a farm at all?' The complete pre-reading part of one interaction demonstrated this use of comprehension questions.

Teacher	What's the book called?
	Do you remember?
Anne	The Friendly Farmer.
Teacher	The Friendly Farmer.
	Where have we got up to now?
	What's the name of the two children in the story?
Anne	Simon and Elizabeth.
Teacher	Elizabeth.
	And where are they going?
Anne	To the farm.
Teacher	What does that word say?
	[pause]
	Simon and Elizabeth are going to?
Anne	Visit.
Teacher	Visit a farm.
	Where was the farm?
	In the town or the country?
Anne	Country.
Teacher	In the country.
	Have you been on a farm at all?
Anne	Yes.
Teacher	You have.
Anne	I have been loads of times.

	My friend works on a farm.
Teacher	How many times have they been to a farm?
Anne	Once.
Teacher	How do you know?
	How do you know they have been only once?
Anne	Because they ask can we see things.
Teacher	Yes.
	Can we read this and it might tell us.

Often with a younger reader the questioning might quite simply ask the child to consider a picture related to the text to be read and therefore to prepare him for the task in hand. That is he would be aware of the context of the reading before he began to read and thus be able to anticipate part of the text.

Teacher	Now what are the mummy and daddy doing in the picture?
Brian	Washing the car.
Teacher	Washing the car.
	Where's the word wash.
	Can you find it?
Brian	Wash.
Teacher	That's right.
	Have you got a car at home?
	And do you help to wash it?
Brian	Yes.
Teacher	Right.
	Let's see if you can read this page.

The questions used prior to the child beginning to read from the text can be an important element of the total interaction. In certain cases the teacher may want to get the child reading immediately, possibly with the purpose of giving adequate time for practice and to diagnose the miscues the child is making. However, on many occasions the teacher will want to question the child about previously unknown words; aspects of phonics; the text to be read through reference to an illustration; or other comprehension questions related to a text which has been previously read. This, then, leads to a substantial pre HCR, as suggested in Chapter 1. Often the questions will attempt to relate the text to the child's own experiences. Each of these forms of questioning helps to prepare the child for the text to be read. It is the reading of the text and the teacher's response to that reading which will form the basis of the next chapter.

Chapter four

Hearing a child read

As soon as a child begins to read it is likely that he will deviate from the text at various points. He will produce an error or miscue, as it might be more commonly referred to now, following K.S. Goodman (1967). An error, as Goodman argued, suggested that the reader does not know something or is careless in his application of what he knows. A miscue implies that the reader has used the available information but on that occasion given too much weight to a particular cueing system.

How should the teacher respond to the miscues that are made? She will need to have some awareness of the variety of miscues that are produced and of the cuing systems which the child is utilizing. Although there are many ways of categorizing the miscues that are produced, for classroom purposes seven main categories may be noted. They are those of substitution, insertion, omission, self-correction, repetition, hesitation, and sounding out.

1 Substitution: this is evident when the reader provides a word, or non-word, which is not the text word, e.g
'Can we see them? said (says) Simon.'

2 Insertion: the reader provides an additional word which is not part of the text, e.g.
'I made the hair **by** myself, says Elizabeth.'

3 Omission: the reader leaves out a text word during his oral reading, e.g.
'Elizabeth has got her shells and her *new* yellow ball.'

4 Self-correction: the reader corrects an error without any help or intervention from the teacher, e.g.
'You saw her – their foot marks by the pond.'

5 Repetition: the reader repeats part of the text, e.g
'He–He will make them fly.'

6 Hesitation: the reader pauses before a word, e.g.
'Can I hide//here, Dad?'

7 Sounding out: the reader makes an attempt at a word through the use of graphophonic knowledge, e.g.
'She is /n/–/n/– not a big doll she is a little one.'

Many of these miscue types may require no response from the teacher. Thus as Cliff Moon argued (NATE 1985), insertions and omissions are often made by readers who are actively involved with the text and they may be producing a more flowing style than is printed. Often the insertions and omissions will not disrupt the meaning and therefore intervention may not be required. Similarly short hesitations, repetitions, or self-corrections may indicate a textual weakness rather than a problem of the reader. Or those miscues may be indicative of the reader's gaining time to consider the text and the meaning of the particular passage. Sounding-out may occur relatively infrequently but require some guidance towards that phonic analysis or the meaning of the text.

Substitutions are the only miscues not so far commented upon. These miscues are actually the most frequently produced by young readers and, of course, they contain the most information about the cue system or systems that the reader may have been utilizing as he reads. The nature of the substitution may well determine how the teacher responds, if at all, to the reader. First, however, it requires some understanding of miscue analysis. At the simplest level this entails a knowledge of the three cueing systems which have been suggested by Goodman (1973). He indicated that readers utilize graphophonic, syntactic, and semantic cueing systems. In the graphophonic cues the reader responds to the graphic sequences and may use correspondences between these graphic sequences and the phonological systems of his dialect.

John   Look I have me (made) the tea
                                    for you.

The miscue in this example suggests the reader has used the graphophonic cues, although not fully, first letter similarity is particularly evident. However, he has largely ignored the sentence structure, syntactic cue, and meaning, semantic cue, in reading 'me' for the text word 'made'. At other times the reader may use the contextual cues, syntactic and semantic, but not the graphophonic.

Ian   The shop keeper
                                    will take the money
                                    and give you a (the) doll.

There is no apparent use of graphophonic information in this example as the reader says 'a' for 'the'. However, the miscue would appear to use syntactic and semantic information. The two examples above would seem to suggest that miscues are produced because the reader has used either the graphophonic or the syntactic and semantic. This is not the case. As Goodman (1973) argues, the 'cue systems are used simultaneously and interdependently'. This leads the child to make not only substitutions as already shown but also substitutions which may make use of each of the cue systems.

Jane   And at one corner
                                    there was a little white house
                                    with–with a yellow roof
                                    and a yellow door.
                                    Johnny–Johnny–Johnny and–Johnny
                                              and Jennifer Yellow hat

                                    lived–lived there.
                                    Here–Here are Jenny–Johnny and
                                                     Jennifer.
                                    One day, a (an) old man and
                                    a little white–little cat came to
                                    The Village with Three Corners.
                                    The little–The old man looked at the
                                                         village.
                                    Stop (Stay) here, little cat,
                                    he said.

I will go (come) – I will move (come)
back // for you, one day.

Jane's reading indicated the variety of miscues that might appear during a read. The substitutions provide a considerable insight about Jane's use of cue systems. At least two of these substitutions, 'a' (an) and 'Stop' (Stay), indicate that Jane may indeed have been using graphophonic, syntactic, and semantic cues simultaneously and interdependently.

If the teacher is aware of the possibilities of miscue analysis, her hearing of a child read may become more sensitive as she considers 'Why did he read that?' (Goodacre 1976). In addition, of course, in response to the miscue the teacher may ask, 'How shall I respond to his reading?' It is to this second question in particular that we shall now turn.

When the reader miscues a word

Once the child begins to read from the text, miscues are likely to be made which will make a demand upon the teacher to decide upon a response. As a first reaction to a miscue it might be appropriate for the teacher to wait. This waiting allows time for the child to self-correct, an important attribute of reading development (Clay 1979). Indeed, Goodman (1965) indicated that in view of the way in which children frequently self-correct, then correcting them may be unnecessary and undesirable. Pehrsson's (1974) investigation which was in part designed to explore whether a teacher helps a child to understand better what he reads by correcting him during the process of oral reading, would appear to support Goodman's view. Pehrsson's results suggest that a child reads better (rate of reading and comprehension) when requested to read for meaning and when he is not interrupted during the reading process. At the very least, therefore, waiting in order to allow time for the child to self-correct would seem to be appropriate.

Colin

Look at the necklace
said Big Red Wing.
It may help you to find where
Sun Dew has gone.
The string is not // filled.

Teacher   Good boy.

The child hesitated // for 12 seconds before reading the word 'filled'. By waiting, the teacher gave the child time to consider, by whatever means, and then self-correct. A more immediate response by the teacher would have denied this opportunity for the child to develop his reading strategies (Glynn 1980). A 12-second wait will entail a substantial silence! It is, however, not being argued that 12 seconds should become a norm but it is apparent that the teacher will need to demonstrate a willingness to wait following a miscue, thus giving the child the opportunity to consider the available cues and self-correct.

There were, however, other occasions in the HCR project when a child reading miscued but the teacher did not respond. This might have occurred when the teacher's attention was elsewhere and the miscue was not heard. Children will produce sentences with substitutions which, although they might contain elements of graphophonic and/or syntactic similarities with the text, are semantically inappropriate.

Teacher   [aside] Two and two?
Phillip   [reads on]   We with (will) get (go)
Teacher   [aside] Four and two more makes?
Phillip   [reads on]

                        out there and
               up (help) we (our) friends
Teacher   [aside] No, and two more than four?

Had the teacher's attention been with Phillip it is highly probable that the miscues would have received a verbal move from the teacher in order to produce a more acceptable response to the text. The waiting, or missing in this instance, did not lead to a self-correction.

Other substitutions read by the child may not be followed by a self-correction. The teacher must again decide whether to bring the miscue to the child's attention. If the child does not return to the miscue and self-correct should the teacher intervene? A previous example can be provided again that indicated an occasion when the teacher did not intervene despite two miscues of substitution occurring.

Yolande	Mummy (Mother) and Daddy come (came) in.
Teacher	Good.

The miscue 'Mummy' may be a dialect variation from the written text which the teacher ignored. The second miscue retained many of the graphophonic, syntactic, and semantic features of the text word and because it preserved the essential meaning received no teacher response. In this example the fact that the child had been absent from school, and was just restarting oral reading to her teacher, may have influenced the decision to ignore the miscues. However, what is being suggested here is that the teacher might ignore 'good errors' (Hood 1978), such as dialect variations and those which preserve the essential meaning of the text. The teacher would, nevertheless, need to keep a close check on these miscues in order to ensure that they do not remain with the child over a long period of time and become habitual through systematic practice. Clay (1979) reminds us of the need to check on the direction and pace of each child's learning path. A good error may be so only at a certain point in the child's development; later the same error may become a 'not so good error' (to use Hood's terminology). Therefore, although the 'Mummy' (Mother) substitution can be seen as quite acceptable on this occasion, as Yolande read, the teacher might want to respond to that miscue in different ways. First, she might want to talk to Yolande after the reading of the text is complete about the use of the word 'Mummy' for 'Mother'. Of course, that would be dealt with sensitively in order to demonstrate that the substitution was valued but that the text word is actually another word. Or the teacher might want to keep a record of the miscue and to check at a later time, as the child develops as a reader, that the acceptable miscue had not become a 'not so good error'.

Should the teacher respond to a 'not so good error'? Or, more explicitly, if the teacher had been fully tuned in to Phillip's reading above should she have responded to the miscues 'with' (will), 'get' (go), 'up' (help), 'we' (our)? Joyce Hood argued that these miscues do signal a need for instructional attention. This view, rather than a notion of leaving all miscues unattended, would appear to be shared by the teachers in the HCR project.

Colin	said Little Red Wing

		Sun Dew may by (be)
Teacher		may
Colin		be looking for seeds.
Teacher	Yes.	

The miscue 'by' (be), although it has graphophonic similarities, does not preserve the essential meaning of the text. The teacher therefore intervened by use of a word cueing move. She took the child back in the sentence and with rising intonation indicated a question was being asked. What is the next word? In this instance the teacher offered only the word 'may', but more usually might restart the sentence 'Sun Dew may'; nevertheless the miscued word was corrected by Colin. An appropriate maxim for the teacher might be to provide a verbal move to assist the child if the miscue is a 'not so good error'.

Although the above maxim may be a useful starting-point for the teacher confronted by a 'not so good error' it does not provide a complete picture. The analysis of teacher verbal moves indicated that the teacher may use a number of different moves to assist the child. Therefore as has already been suggested at a number of points in this book the teacher may respond with various moves including:

Word cueing: the teacher reads part or all of the sentence leading up to the error but not the misread word. A rising intonation indicates that a question is being asked, namely what is the next word, e.g.

Sally	The boy gets (gives)
Teacher	The boy

Non-response: the teacher decides not to intervene, e.g.

Sally	The boy gets (gives)
Teacher	——
Sally	the dog a bone. Then he goes home.

Negative feedback: the teacher makes a negative comment to indicate that a word has been misread, e.g.

Sally		The boy gets (gives)
Teacher	No.	

Comprehension: the teacher askes a question to encourage the child towards the text word, e.g.

Sally   The boy gets (gives)
Teacher   What is the boy doing?

Provide the word: the teacher provides the word for the reader, e.g.

Sally   The boy gets (gives)
Teacher   gives

Phonic analysis: the teacher suggests to the reader that he should utilize his knowledge of phonics in order to discover the word being misread; the teacher may provide some information, e.g.

Sally   The boy gets (gives)
Teacher   Yes, it does begin with /g/ but it's /gi . . .

Is there a preferred response from each of these possibilities? The non-response to good miscues has already been suggested earlier in this chapter. What if the miscue is a not so good miscue? That question will now be explored.

Teacher response to not go good miscues

As has already been noted in a number of examples a word cueing move is frequently followed by the child's correcting his miscue. In the HCR project an in-depth analysis of almost 400 word cueing moves following a substitution indicated that 85 per cent of those teacher word cueing moves were followed by the child's correcting his miscue. This move does, of course, keep open the use of all three cue systems although it may implicitly stress the use of the contextual cues.

Carl   Fun in the New//
Teacher   [aside] That's okay, right.
                          Fun in the New//
Carl   New House.
Teacher   That's right.

By taking the child back in the text the context is re-emphasized and this, together with the rising intonation by the teacher, would seem to be very helpful to the child. Another feature of this move is the way in which it can be helpful, even though the teacher may not always take the child back to the start of the sentence.

Helen		Help! called the chief of police.
		We are snowed in at the police
		station.
		Would you help us to get out to look
		after
		the people of the town?
		Follow me! said Katy as she began
Teacher	[aside] It is.	
Helen	[reads on]	to push (plough) her way
Teacher		to
Helen		plough
Teacher	Good girl.	
		plough
Helen		her way across town.

The teacher in this example quite simple said 'to' but by rising intonation and within the context of a hearing children read interaction the message was clearly understood, that is you have miscued a word, go back to the word 'to' and try again. Following that simple move Helen, by whatever process, immediately corrected her miscue and was able to carry on reading.

There was evidence from the HCR project to indicate that teachers use word cueing moves following a variety of miscue types. In many instances the move was made following a substitution miscue by the child.

Anita	Jennifer stood by the gate,
	looking at the little black horse.
	She called (could) see
Teacher	She
Anita	She could–could see he was not very
	old.

However, word cueing moves also occurred from time to time after insertions and omissions by the child reading. Thus following the insertion of 'a' by Christopher:

Christopher [reads on]   bunch of balloons was higher than
                                George's head. The–It–It was **a** so
Teacher   It was
Christopher   so high
                                that he couldn't get hold of it.

and of an omission 'bed' while Tracey was reading.

Tracey   I'd better put him to *bed* now.
Teacher   to
Tracey   bed now

A hesitation miscue may also bring forth from the teacher a word cueing move. The child is perhaps being asked not only to continue considering the word in question but also to look again at the preceding words to use contextual clues as well as graphophonic ones.

Steven   Dick said, I can make a //
Teacher   [aside] Right can you write six pence for me.
                          Dick said, I can make a
Steven   house.

As a general strategy, therefore, in response to a miscue which requires attention the teacher might use a word cueing move. The move does seem to help the reader, it is similar to the strategy adopted by able readers (Clay 1979) and it may encourage the child to use that strategy for himself either out aloud or silently (Butler and Clay 1979) in other contexts. He is being encouraged to develop positive reading strategies for future use.

At other times, and particularly for the first word in a sentence, it might be appropriate for the teacher to indicate to the reader an alternative approach. The teachers in the HCR project frequently provided information to children, by use of negative feedback, that quite simply indicated that they had got it wrong.

Ian   Pack (Weigh)
Teacher   No.

Ian   Weigh the packet of tea.
                          You can //

In this move no instructional advice is given to the child although the move does bring to the child's attention the fact that he has miscued. The child is then left to reconsider the miscue and to choose for himself the information from the text which he will utilize. This move may, however, be important as it provides information to the child as to whether his prediction has worked or not worked (Smith 1971). However as Smith also argued, the move is of course offered without punitive overtones. The reader is not being punished for an error, he is being given information so that he will know how his attempts at reading are working out.

Where the teacher fails to, or decides against, providing immediate negative feedback and the reader has read past the miscue then the teacher simply adds the miscued word to her negative feedback move.

Tina   Elizabeth has made the (a) bed.
Teacher   Not the.
Tina   a bed.

Again the message is clearly received by the child. Tina self-corrected and restarted her reading with the correction.

The use of comprehension moves during the interaction, rather than at the beginning or end, was infrequently utilized by the teachers in the HCR project. It may be that the use of such a move, possibly due to its length, may disrupt the child's involvement with the text. Use of the move may, therefore, distract rather than assist the child in attending to the cue systems. However, as it was so infrequently used it is inappropriate to be more definite than suggest the move may be of some use in a limited number of circumstances after the other possible moves have been discounted. An example of this move is provided, however the teacher followed up with a supplementary phonic move and it was not possible to detect which move was most useful to the child.

Craig   for your shop?
                          Can you make a /t/–/t/
Teacher   What sort of shop?

a /t/

Craig   toy shop.

A more extended example of the use of comprehension moves during the reading from the text was evident when Rachel read to her teacher. Here the teacher used a comment by Rachel to discuss the content and ask some questions which were not specifically concerned with reading a word.

Rachel	Yes, it could be, said the man from the garage. It could be the back axle that is broken down.
	It's a breakdown.
Teacher	Yes it is.
	The back axle's important isn't it?
Rachel	Yes.
Teacher	What's happening now do you think?
Rachel	He's tied the rope to the lorry and he's bringing it up the hill to the garage.
Teacher	That's right.
	What's it called when you tie a rope to another car?
	What's that one doing, that one doing?
Rachel	It's towing it up.
Teacher	It's towing it.
	We say it's towing it.
	Because it's pulling it.
	It's got to be a strong rope to do that hasn't it.
Rachel	Oh yes.
	What will you do? asked the driver.

Rather than providing moves which suggest to the child strategies for dealing with the miscued words the teacher may decide, quite simply, to provide the word for the child following his miscue. It may be that the use of such a move on a limited number of occasions does help the child to retain a link with the text. However, if it is used too frequently the child may become dependent upon the teacher as a provider of words.

Sean	were as baby (miscues busy)
Teacher	No.

Sean		busy
	as //	
Teacher		they were as busy
	as //	
		could
Sean		could be

In this example the teacher did attempt preferred moves of negative feedback 'no', and word cueing 'they were as busy as'. However, following those moves she provided the word and Sean carried on reading. Nevertheless the teacher may want to provide the word, particularly at the start of the sentence when other moves may be less applicable, or for early beginning readers in order to help them retain a link with the text. Frequent use of providing the word may, however, lead children to expect the answer if they wait long enough. This move would, Yetta Goodman (1970) argued, hinder the child's attempt to discover reading strategies; it may also discourage self-correction. The extent to which a child may become dependent on the teacher as a provider of words is to be found at the conclusion of an interaction between Jason and his teacher.

Jason	He can //				
Teacher		make			
Jason		make //			
Teacher			Black		
Jason			Black //		
Teacher				Pony	
Jason				Pony //	
Teacher					run
Jason					run //
Teacher						fast
Jason						fast.

It is the teacher who was reading, providing the words, while Jason's role was that of repeating the words which have been uttered. The teacher may have been working very hard but it is doubtful whether Jason was developing appropriate reading strategies.

From time to time teachers may also want to use a phonic analysis move which will indicate to the reader that he should use his knowledge of phonics in order to cue accurately a word which was being miscued. This phonic analysis move occurred most frequently after miscues of substitution or hesitation and emphasized the initial letter(s). This emphasis upon the initial letter(s) does perhaps serve to develop in children the idea that initial letter(s) provide salient clues to the deciphering of words (Marchbanks and Levin 1965). Biemiller (1970), following his study of oral reading errors, argued the need to encourage children to use graphic information as much as possible in order to develop from the earlier stages of reading development which suggested a predominant use of contextual information. The move may be useful for that reason.

Jason	[reads on]	a big surprise on the farm.
		Look here Jane, said Dick.
		All the nuts fell //
Teacher	[aside]	Right colour that page before you go on to the next one.

/f/

| Jason | from the tree. |
| Teacher | Good. |

The most frequently used phonic analysis moves by the teacher are those which specifically utter the initial letter(s) as indicated with Jason or, as in the case of Richard, where the teacher asks, 'What is the first sound?'

Richard	He said, //
Teacher	[aside] Which piece is missing?
	What's the first sound?
Richard	/c/–can I help my–help you?
	Oh, yes!

Only in very few instances did any of the teachers change from these phonic analysis moves to moves which refer to so called 'phonic rules'.

Colin	They–They could not see Sun Dew
	We will look near that pin (pine)
Teacher	Now what does that e do?
Colin	pine tree.
Teacher	Good boy.

The three examples of phonic analysis moves indicate that they might be helpful to a child and enable him to cue a previously miscued word. The success rate, in the HCR project, following the phonic analysis move was, however, less than 50 per cent. And this move might best be used with considerable caution. However a further example demonstrates how a child appeared to use a phonic analysis move as an aid to reading a word accurately.

Nicky	One day, Mr Red-hat
	came up the hill,
	Up–Old man, he cried,
	You will have to go.
	You must go down
	to the foot of the hill //
Teacher	/f/
Nicky	/f/–/or/–for the wind is coming.

Nicky used the phonic information which the teacher provides: /f/. In addition he sounded out the rest of the word /or/ and then cued the word 'for'. Nevertheless at other times – approximately 25 per cent in the HCR project – the teacher had to provide further phonic analysis moves to enable the child to cue the word. The first phonic analysis move was usually insufficient to help the reader.

Ian		Can you buy tea
		at your shop?
		Buy a packet of tea
		//
Teacher	What's this sound?	
Ian		/f/
Teacher		/fr/
Ian		from the shop.
		Weigh the tea (packet)

Inevitably then there were occasions when this emphasis upon phonics did not help the child. Sean may 'know his sounds' but this did not necessarily lead to a synthesis of sounds into an appropriate word.

Sean	Down, down came the house!
	It came down on Dick and Tom.

	It came down on Jane and Susan.	
	It came down on Sally, and	
	it came down on little Tim.	
	My, my! laughed Mother.	
	I can see some bumps up (under)	
Teacher	Not up.	
	Say the sounds to me.	
	What's the first sound?	
Sean		/u/
Teacher	That's right.	
Sean		/n/
Teacher		/n/
Sean		/d/ /e/ /r/–up
		(under)
Teacher		under
Sean		under this

Clearly it can be argued that these phonic analysis moves are far more restrictive than the word cueing move. The phonic analysis move is directing a child to graphophonic cue systems, therefore limiting the use of other cue systems, whereas the word cueing move, while not denying the possible use of graphophonic systems, might also suggest the syntactic and semantic systems. It is interesting to speculate on Peter's response below had a word cueing move been utilized instead of the phonic analysis move: 'What's the first sound?'

Peter		Roger Red hat
		Had a red ball.
		A little /wh/
Teacher		white
Peter		white dog came (went) by.
Teacher	Not came by.	
	What's the first sound?	
Peter	I don't know.	

An important feature of the various moves used by the teachers was the way in which word cueing, negative feedback, and indeed providing the word could all be used to support the reader and create virtually no disruption to the reading. Of course, providing the word may do less to encourage positive reading strategies but it is less disruptive to the reader than moves of comprehension or phonic analysis. An important aim for the teacher is to keep the child involved with text. Therefore, there will also be non-verbal gestures of pointing, smiling, grimacing, and so on which will be used to keep the child reading and which will occur in the interaction in a manner which does not disrupt the activity. Although very little attention is given to non-verbal aspects in this book it is recognized that these gestures will be used as the teacher hears a child read. Nevertheless it may be the verbal moves which can be more informative for the reader as the teacher guides and support the child.

Teacher providing positive feedback

As the child reads, self-corrects, corrects his miscues following a teacher move, and completes his reading, opportunities will arise for the teacher to provide information that he is right. She will therefore be acting again as an information provider (Smith 1971). However, the information would appear as positive feedback and, therefore, not only would provide information but also would give praise and encouragement to the child. Glynn (1980) stated quite clearly when this positive feedback should be given. He suggested providing praise contingent upon correct performance (for example sentences or pages read correctly), self-correction of errors, and error correction following a prompt. The teachers did use positive feedback at certain predictable moments in the HCR project. Indeed these predictable moments were similar to those put forward by Glynn. They were used often to confirm a child's self-correction or miscue correction following a teacher move. They were also used to praise correct performance: a sentence read in the case of the weakest readers and a page read in the case of the more able readers. The use of positive feedback appeared to provide a dual message, 'Yes, you are reading correctly', and also, 'Keep on reading'. Finally, they were used to praise the child upon the completion of his read. These moves appeared to be helpful to the child and act as an encouragement in his reading. Others might argue that this use of positive feedback provides useful information to the child (Smith 1971) or appropriate reinforcement (Skinner 1968). In addition, like other teacher moves, providing it is uttered in a minimum form, such as 'yes', 'mm', it will minimize disruption to the child as he reads. If the teacher is attempting to be supportive of the child, that encouragement surely needs to be given in a manner that does not distract the child's attention away from the text. A number of interactions provided examples of such encouragement and information. First, James received positive feedback as he self-corrected following a hesitation. The use of a short utterance to provide positive feedback enabled James to carry on reading.

James	She does not // /h/ /ho/ – hold
Teacher	Good.
James	on
	with her hand.
	Now look at Penny.
Teacher	Mm.

Second, the teacher may provide the positive feedback to confirm a child's miscue correction following a teacher verbal move, in this instance with Mark a combined negative feedback and word cueing move.

Mark	all came (come)
Teacher	No.
	They all
Mark	come
Teacher	That's it.

The third example of positive feedback occurred where James read correctly a line/sentence 'Look at Susan, said Peter' and again 'See Susan flying'. This provision of feedback after such a small amount of reading was provided, particularly for the weakest readers, as perceived by the teacher. The message appeared to be twofold. The child was told that his reading was appropriate and also was asked to continue reading. Importantly, however, the child with limited reading attainment is informed that his predictions of the printed page are correct.

James	Look at Susan, said Peter.
Teacher	Mm.
James	See Susan flying.
Teacher	Yes.

Fourth, a reader received positive feedback at the end of a page and/or his complete reading interaction. Although most children will receive positive feedback at this point the more able readers might have had to read a complete page or pages before receiving their first positive feedback from the teacher.

Brett, who was perceived by the teacher as an able reader, had to read a complete page before receiving positive feedback.

Brett	That was harder then–than pulling houses. She can do anything, said one man. When the snow comes, Katy will have to push snow off the roads, said another. That will be harder than anything that she will have done all summer. Katy will get along all right, said one of the men. The harder the work she has to do the better she likes it.
Teacher	Good boy, Brett.

Although most frequently the teacher will provide the positive feedback in a short form to minimize the interruption to the child's reading, as a variation she may repeat the child's last word or words to indicate that he is reading accurately.

Jason	No, no, no, said Ellen. Now let Dick and //
Teacher	Peter–Peter
Jason	Peter guess.
Teacher	guess.

The teacher followed Jason's 'guess' with her own 'guess' and with appropriate intonation she informed Jason that he was reading accurately. However, it is possible for a child to misinterpret this message of positive feedback and, perhaps, see it instead as a provision of a word.

Steven		in it.
Teacher		it.
Steven	I said it.	
Teacher	Oh sorry.	
	Right.	
Steven		Tim can play in it.

In this case the teacher repaired the interaction with an apology and Steven continued to read.

An interesting feature of the use of positive feedback in the HCR project was that children regarded by their teacher as the weakest readers received most positive, as well as negative, feedback. Part of the explanation for that was that weakest readers may receive feedback after a line or sentence of reading whereas ablest readers may have to read a complete page before receiving feedback. It may also be the case that weakest readers miscue more frequently, thus creating the opportunity for negative feedback or other moves to occur and also for positive feedback after they have corrected their miscue.

Another explanation may be that weakest readers received most feedback due to an awareness by the teachers that the weakest readers required most information in order to begin to develop rules about reading (Smith 1971). Or it may be that the teachers were using a sophisticated form of intermittent reinforcement in which for the ablest readers there was an increase in the number of responses per reinforcement (Skinner 1968). Yet again it might be that the teachers recognized different purposes for hearing children read. This might range from checking on comprehension with the ablest readers to imparting a feeling of success to the weakest readers (Moyle 1968). Whatever the explanation may be, it can be noted that the weakest readers in the HCR project did receive more positive feedback per read than either average or ablest readers. It might, therefore, be argued that the Matthew effect (he that hath shall be given: the able receive more support) in the classroom (Burstall 1978) did not occur during the hearing children read interactions in the HCR project. Indeed a reverse Matthew effect of the weakest receiving most praise and encouragement was indicated.

Directions in order to sustain the interaction

One of the most frequently utilized teacher verbal moves was that of direction. That move is used to direct and control the interaction. The move in various forms indicated not only the beginning of the read, by calling the name of the child to read, but also, as we shall see, directed the length, pace, and development of the read as well as the completion.

As we have already noted, the child was called to his teacher's desk to read and various questons might be asked of him prior to commencing his reading. However the teacher would most usually direct when the reading was to begin.

| Teacher | Off you go, Richard. |
| Richard | A man came up the street. |

That move to commence reading, however, might quite simply be a marker (Sinclair and Coulthard 1975). Okay, now, and right are examples of markers which are used to indicate a boundary in, for instance, a conversation. In the classroom such words would appear to indicate quite clearly to the child that a boundary had been reached and suggested that he should start reading.

Teacher	Right.
Nicky	The little old man
	looked out of the window.
	Let the wind come! he cried.

The teacher may perceive miscues uttered by a child as occuring owing to reading too quickly. She might therefore provide moves not only to indicate that a miscue has been made, 'No', but also to direct a change of pace.

Richard	The princess is running because
	(back)
Teacher	No.
	Go slower.

In the above example the suggestion to read slower would be based on the teacher's view that the miscue occurred owing to recoding the printed words too quickly, that is without paying sufficient attention to the graphophonic cueing system. On other occasions the request came as a child read the words accurately but perhaps at a rhythm which suggested that full meaning was not being extracted. Specifically the punctuation of the passage was being ignored.

Mark   At last the hundred years were over
                                          and
                       one day the king–the son of the king
                                  of that
                       country came by on his horse. He
                                 saw the
                       great

Teacher   No.
           Let's have it a bit slowly
                                 came by on his horse.
           Stop
                                           He saw

Mark   He saw
                     the
                     great castle with its huge towers.

Within the interaction the teacher was also likely to determine the length of the reading, most usually in terms of the number of pages to be read.

Neil   She may have gone to the wood
                       for red seeds.
Teacher   Yes.
           Next page.
Neil   Big Red Wing and Little Red Wing

The direction to determine the number of pages read would also be used finally, of course, when the teacher used a direction move in order to inform the child that the interaction was being concluded.

Jan   for you,
                     one day.
Teacher   Good girl.
           We'll stop there.

As with the start of a read so too at the finish the teacher might use only a single word marker to indicate to the child that the interaction was complete.

Peter		with the ball.
Teacher	Okay.	
	Right.	

Although it may be possible to be critical of the nature of the teacher–pupil relationship where the teacher is directing, controlling, and evaluating within hearing children read (Hale 1980), nevertheless an element of direction may be required in order for the child to perceive the nature and development of such interactions. The directions do apparently serve to sustain the interaction and provide it with a structure. However, although directions may be required they should not be seen as providing a mechanistic control of the interaction; they are there to guide the interaction. The directions should not act as a barrier to a positive social relationship's being established within the activity.

Social relationships

It has already been suggested that the teacher needs to provide a well-organized classroom in order to minimize distractions, and teacher asides, and therefore to permit meaningful interactions to occur. Furthermore, the teacher needs to give careful thought to the variety of strategies that are used in response to the reader's miscues. Additionally the teacher needs to demonstrate by an overall positive accepting attitude towards the reader that a genuine shared activity is taking place. Bettelheim and Zelan (1982) argued that when offered an appropriate social relationship children will interrupt their own reading in order to talk about the text and to give their direct and indirect reactions to it. A young child may be unlikely to comment upon his reading of the text if the teacher is emphasizing accurate reading, responding to other children or suggesting that the interaction is severely constrained by time. However, if in contrast the teacher is sharing the text with an emphasis upon meaning, attending to the child, allowing time for the interaction to be completed in a natural manner, and in general suggesting an empathy with the reader, then the child might feel safe enough to express his thoughts about and reactions to what he is reading by interrupting from time to time and talking to his teacher.

In the HCR project one particular in-depth analysis of Brian reading to his teacher throughout a school year demonstrated how a reader would feel free to initiate interruptions to talk about his reading or the text. Furthermore the analysis noted how the teacher would accept and frequently use those reader initiations as a basis for discussion. It was noted that Brian interrupted his reading to comment upon words, the text, and the illustrations, to relate to personal experiences and to indicate a concern for the teacher's welfare.

Brian, then, did interrupt and comment upon words which were creating uncertainties. In one instance Brian hesitated // before the word 'after' and then sought confirmation from the teacher that he had previously read the word.

Brian   Look at the coaches.
                               Can you count the coaches
                               can–or–on the long train?
                               They are–They all come //
I had that word in the other book didn't I?
Teacher   Yes.
                               They all come

At other times in his concern about a word Brian would quite simply interrupt to correct his miscue and indicate verbally that he was wrong.

Brian   He–Have you a shop at school
                               Draw the–Draw a–Draw a princess
                                         (picture)
           No it isn't princess.
Teacher   It does begin with a /p/.
                       Draw a
Brian   picture of your shop.

Sometimes the word which created a problem may have been a new word. Brian might and did use the graphophonic, syntactic, and semantic cue systems to read words. However in the next example, after a hesitation in front of the word 'tiger', Brian commented upon the fact that he was being confronted by a new word. Possibly he was finding it difficult to read that particular word, therefore he told his teacher that it was a new word, perhaps in the hope of getting some assistance.

Brian	The children are playing
	in the long grass.
	Come and hide, says Elizabeth.
	Can you see me – Can you see me
	Simon?
	said – Come and hide in the long
	grass.
	He is a //
	That's a new word.
Teacher	Yes.
	So he is a ?
Brian	It is a new word.
Teacher	It is a new word.
	So what's he pretending to be?
	He is a tiger.
	He's pretending to be a tiger.
Brian	tiger.
	Look at me, he says.
	I am a tiger, a big tiger.

Another example to indicate Brian's interruptions in front of a word creating a problem was noted where Brian read 'naughty' (hungry); however, he subsequently interrupted to inform his teacher that he had been 'going to say nosey'. It is not inappropriate to speculate that the preceding text might have encouraged him to think that 'nosey' would be a reasonable choice.

Brian	Look, there is the (a) fire engine
	coming down–down the street. It is
	going fast.
	All the people are coming out to see
	it.
	I am naughty (hungry)
Teacher	No.
Brian	I am
	I was going to say nosey.
Teacher	I am
	What does it begin with?
Brian	hungry,
Teacher	That's right.

Brian   says Simon.
                      Are you hungry, Elizabeth?

In that example not only was Brian interrupting to talk about a word
but also he was in part commenting upon the text. Indeed a second
reason for Brian to interrupt his reading was to make comment upon
the text. For instance Brian's involvement and enjoyment of the text
led him at one point to laugh and subsequently he commented on the
story. Following the comment he immediately restarted his reading.
He was, perhaps, too intent upon reading to become involved in a
dialogue with the teacher. After completing the paragraph he restated
his comment and, therefore, invited a response from the teacher.

Brian   Next–Next they find a house made
                                of–a house made of jelly.
           Ha, ha!
                                This will not do–This will not do,
                                says one of the little kittens. The
                                children will eat it all up–
           And it will wobble!
                                                    all up and then
                                                      there will be
                      no house left.
           And it would wobble.
Teacher   It would wobble.
           Go on then.

Another example where Brian commented upon the text was when he
indicated a degree of incredulity with the story.

Brian   The cook and the pilot jumped (jump)
                                over the side of the boat. A–The water
                                is very cold and they paddled (paddle)
                                in the waves. You see, says the pilot,
                                we–we are all right after all, says–Yes,
                                says the cook, and what about break-
                                fast? It–it is all right for you. I did not
                                have my breakfast. I have some sand-
                                wiches there–here says the pilot. I put
                                them under my hat and they did not
                                get wet.

74

Of course they would!

Teacher   Why.

Brian   When he jumped in.

Brian also interrupted his reading to comment upon the illustrations which were alongside the text. This might be to question the accuracy of the picture or to check upon the text by relating the storyline to the picture;

Brian   Got you! he said (says). I said I will
                                            (would)

Teacher   I

Brian   I
                    would catch you and
                    I have.

He hasn't got anybody yet.

Teacher   He hasn't got him yet has he?

Brian   Look, there he is.
                    No says the Giant. You will not catch
                    me. I am too big for you to catch. You–
                    See how little you are. You will not
                    catch me. No one can catch me.

In general a teacher may wish to question the child about the text and relate the text to his personal experiences. However the child might also wish to do this. Thus Brian provided an interruption to his reading in order to relate the text to his own personal experiences. In this instance an experience which was shared with the teacher.

Brian   Ducks in the mud!
                    Ducks in the mud!
                    Let–Left, right! Left, right! They walk
                                  down in–in
                    (to) the pond. Quack! Quack! they go.
                    Down they go into–in the water, under
                                  the weed.
          We need weed.

Teacher   We do need weed for our frog.

Finally, during one interaction it was obvious that the teacher was suffering from a hoarse throat. However, during the course of the interaction she did manage to improve her voice projection, at least to some extent. This led to an interruption from Brian which indicated a concern for the teacher's welfare (as well as demonstrating Brian's development as a language user).

Brian	Tell me what you did in the play-house.
	Let me see what you have made.
Teacher	Lovely.
	The word tell isn't it.
	The /e/ sound.
	This letter gives the /e/ sound.
Brian	Oh, your voice is getting weller.

Although the few extracts from interactions which have been included above indicate that Brian as a reader may have felt sufficiently secure within the social relationships of the interaction to feel free to comment upon his reading and the text, it may only be by listening to such interactions and capturing the subtleties of intonation that the empathy of teacher and child can be fully appreciated. Nevertheless the impression given is that the teacher has to convey by her every action and word that a genuine shared activity is in progress.

This chapter has considered the teacher responses to the child as he reads. It does suggest that the teacher's role while she hears a child read is both complex and important. She needs to organize the classroom, to observe, diagnose, and instruct on the spot as well as to provide an appropriate relationship of shared endeavour. Her responses would appear to help the child towards developing his reading strategies and encourage interest and enjoyment of reading. The analysis would not support the notion that hearing a child reading is in any way suggestive of a passive role for the listener. To the contrary the analysis indicates an active role with important consequences for initial reading development and perhaps for subsequent involvement in reading in later years.

The suggestions for helping the reader, which have been put forward in this chapter, are brought together in some guidelines in Chapter 6. However, prior to that, the next chapter examines the way in which the interaction was brought to completion by many of the teachers in the HCR project.

Chapter five

Completing the interaction

After the child has completed his reading of the text the teacher may decide to spend some time questioning him about his reading. On other occasions she may complete the interaction as the child finishes his read. Within the structure of the interaction, as we noted in Chapter 1, there will be a post HCR element of varying length.

A child who has read with some competence may be provided with postive feedback and the interaction concluded. Thus when Lee read to his teacher the post HCR element was very short.

Lee	There was a big ring and a parade of horses go–going round. There were big horses and little horses. There were black horses and white horses.
Teacher	Thank you, Lee. Well done.

Of course, seen in isolation that short contribution from the teacher would appear to be somewhat superficial. Would it contribute to the child's reading development and view of reading? Does it demonstrate a genuine shared activity? It does appear that the teacher has lost the opportunity for an exchange about the text or the child's view of the text. However, in the wider context of hearing Lee read on a regular basis throughout the school year and having substantial exchanges on other occasions then perhaps that short conclusion may not have been so inappropriate. Certainly at other times the teacher would devote time to questioning the child as the read was completed. As Helen finished her read this occurred. In this instance Helen's reading had been quite accurate (93 per cent word accuracy). However, the teacher spent some time asking questions about the text and therefore a more lengthy post HCR was evident.

Helen	Thank you! called the chief of police. Great (Glad)
Teacher	No.
Helen	Glad to help! said the big red tractor.
Teacher	That's right. Who called for help?
Helen	The police.
Teacher	The police. Why did they call for help?
Helen	Because the roads were covered with ice.
Teacher	With ice and snow. And who came to help them?
Helen	Katy.
Teacher	And what did she do?
Helen	She pushed the snow away.
Teacher	That's right she pushed the snow away. Good girl.

Helen was questioned to assess her comprehension of the text. However, the teacher might question a child in order to develop other aspects of the interaction.

Teacher questions at the end of a read

What sort of questions might the teacher ask as the child completes his read? First, there may be questions which attempt to relate the text to the child's own experience. Second, there are, as we have already noted, questions which are used to determine the child's comprehension of the text. Third, the child may be questioned about specific words which he has previously miscued. The teacher will often test the child to see if this previously miscued word, in context, is now known out of context, often as part of a list on the child's reading card. However, it needs to be recognized that the demand of reading a word from a list will be quite different from reading the word in context. The

78

syntactic and semantic cues will no longer be available and the task may, therefore, be more difficult for the reader. Fourth, the teacher may provide some phonics teaching based upon her earlier diagnosis of a need as the child was reading.

In the example provided below, John has read the sentence 'I don't like climbing trees' from the text. The teacher used the opportunity provided by that sentence to ask John a question about his own preferences. This was then developed into a discussion of his past experience.

John	I don't like climbing trees.
	I–And look at all that mud **on**
Teacher	Not on.
	. And look at all that mud.
John	That boy has mud–mud all over him!
	Percy went on and Billy had to go
	too.
Teacher	Do you like climbing trees?
John	Yes.
Teacher	Yes you do because you once wrote about it didn't you, climbing trees? Dangerous that, you have to take care, you have to be careful.
John	I look for trees like that.
Teacher	With a shape so that you can get your foot in easily. Is that what you do?
	Do you go up high?
John	In Epping Forest I went round with my Dad and there's this tree and there's branches sticking out the side and it's like steps you just walk up.
Teacher	Was it like a playhouse there or did you make one?
John	No we just used the trees.
Teacher	That sounds nice, I like the idea of that.

By relating the text to John's own experiences the teacher seemed to be able to get a more extended utterance from him. This was certainly so in this instance. At other times decisions were made to question the reader about his comprehension of the text. At one level this might be to check on word meanings.

Helen	I got the mail from the post office

	to the railway station.
	I helped get the telephone lines up.
	Now I'm going to help you.
	Come on! It won't take long
	to get – to get these (those) water
	pipes working.
	And off went Katy
Teacher	[aside] Simon.
Helen	[reads on]
	followed by the men
	and the trucks from the water works.
	She took them to the people who had
	trouble with–with water pipes.
Teacher	Very nicely read.
	Em, Katy went to get the mail didn't she?
	What is the mail?
	Can you tell me?
Helen	Letters and parcels.
Teacher	Good girl, letters and parcels.
	That's right.
	Good girl.
	Right.
	Off you go.

However, at other times the comprehension questions were used to assess the extent to which the child had understood the passage being read.

Kerry	Fifth Brother made a house for
	himself.
	He made it without windows because
	he didn't need any air.
	There was just one thing that troubled
	the five brothers.
Teacher	[aside] Natalie.
Kerry	[reads on]
	The people kept
	asking
	First Brother to tell how he caught
	fish.

	But First Brother began to see that he would have to tell or get into trouble.
Teacher	Thank you very much. What was the one thing that troubled the brothers?
Kerry	The man – umh – kept asking first brother how to show him to fish.
Teacher	That's right. Yes so what did – What did First Brother think they would have to do?
Kerry	He would have to show them or he would get into trouble.
Teacher	He would wouldn't he? Yes. Good girl, Kerry. Thank you.

This type of questioning occurred with some frequency in the HCR project. The questions were however concerned with literal comprehension (Barrett 1968) and it might be appropriate to consider whether questions could be asked of the child which create a demand for inference. It might be argued that this was what the teacher was doing as Lisa completed her reading.

Lisa	When he is a big horse he will eat it.
Teacher	He says there, look. He didn't nip me. And she likes to feel that he's taking the hay from her hand. What would you think it would feel like?
Lisa	Rough.
Teacher	Do you think it would be rough? A horse's mouth is ever so soft. It's lips are soft. I think it would feel tickly.

Although the demand here might have been for inference, another feature of this interaction, as it was closed, was the way in which the teacher was dominating the use of language. The opportunity for the child to explore ideas through language was lost as the teacher began to provide information. The awareness of a teacher about the sort of questions to be asked may be insufficient. She will also need to consider what opportunities the questions provide for the child to use language.

The questions, as has already been suggested, may be of a more mechanical nature. They might be used to test the child about previously miscued words.

Susannah	I know what is a good colour
	for that little house, said Peter.
	White is just the colour for it.
Teacher	Well done, Susannah.
	Good girl.
	What's this word [on pupil's reading card]?
Susannah	Could.
Teacher	Could.
	You've got it right and this one?
Susannah	Which.
Teacher	Which.
	Right.
	Well done.

Susannah was questioned about word recognition out of context. That is she had to recognize words from a word list on her reading card, the word list having been developed from previously miscued words. This was a frequently noted practice in the HCR project, where teachers were testing word recognition. However, an alternative strategy was for the teacher to assess the words in context.

Tina	You must be good children
	and good (go)
Teacher	Not good.
Tina	go to bed.
Teacher	Good girl.
	You read extremely well indeed.
	Good girl.
	Emh – find me the word taking.
Tina	Taking.
Teacher	Good girl.
	Find me the word putting.
Tina	Putting.

Teacher   Good.
              Find me the word family.
              You read that beautifully.

This strategy may be helpful to a child as it would enable him to use all the cueing systems in order to find the word. Later the teacher might want to see if the word can be read out of context.

In contrast an interaction may be completed with the teacher emphasizing phonics. The reader may miscue a word during his reading of the text and the miscued word might be used subsequently to develop an aspect of phonics.

James   for Penny.
Teacher   Good boy.
              That was a very difficult page wasn't it, eh?
              Now it's just this little one.
              /t/
James   take.
Teacher   take.
              Take away the /t/ and put in this letter what do we get?
James   make.
Teacher   Take away the /m/ and put in that letter.
James   make – bake.
Teacher   Take away the /b/ and now put in this letter.
James   cake.
Teacher   cake.
              Well done, James.

The above example may be helpful to James. First, it reminds him of the graphophonic cueing system and how that might be used to decode words. Second, drawing attention to the graphophonic cues outside the actual reading of the text may be less disruptive to the reader than using such strategies to support his reading of a passage.

The areas which were questioned by the teachers in the HCR project related quite clearly to the areas which Veatch (1978) postulated should be examined during individual conferences, namely personal identification, comprehension skills, and mechanical skills. Veatch subsequently put forward an extensive list of questions that might be asked under each heading. However, she did not suggest that all the questions should be asked within a single conference. Nor did she argue that the areas needed to be explored in a set order. She indicated that it is the depth to which an area is explored which might be best for reading growth. It might, therefore, be appropriate for the teacher to question the child on personal experiences, comprehension, and/or word recognition and phonics as each relate to the text. The questioning might best attempt to explore in depth specific aspects rather than to deal superficially with numerous aspects of the text.

The end of the interaction

As the interaction is brought to a close it wouold seem apposite that a closing welfare move is provided. This would provide a logical balance to the opening welfare move and act to confirm the relationship that was developed during the interaction.

Helen	[reads on]	or iron and twelve pounds of steel, and a smith to hammer and a smith to hold.
Teacher		Well done. You are getting on well with this book, Helen. Would you like to finish to the end of the story?
Helen		Yes.
Teacher		I think you could manage that. Good girl. Well done, Helen.

The interaction with Helen was clearly but not abruptly concluded by the teacher and the child was both praised as well as having her opinion sought. A sequence of closing moves including positive feedback and welfare moves might therefore be appropriate. Of course, in this closing sequence no questions were asked and these might logically be added prior to the sequence. However, the important point was that the interaction was completed in a friendly and unhurried manner despite the considerable number of tasks that the teacher was likely to have before her as she attempted to provide worthwhile learning experiences for all the children in the class.

Chapter six

Some guidelines for hearing a child read

During the course of the discussion of the various elements which constitute the hearing children read interaction it will have been noted that value judgements as to what might be considered 'good' practice were indicated. Those various suggestions which have been put forward can be brought together to provide guidelines for a teacher when hearing children read. Perhaps the main danger in providing such a list is that it might be regarded as a checklist of points to be covered. This is not its purpose; it is not meant to be totally prescriptive. Within the context of the classroom, together with an individual child, the teacher will need to adjust according to her professional judgements and use those suggestions which appear to be most relevant. However, the list might provide a framework from which those judgements can be made. The list was constructed on the basis of what teachers actually do when hearing children read, some evaluation as to what appeared to be helpful to each child, as well as comments that have been made by other authors who have considered this interaction (e.g. NATE 1985).

This list will also have some relevance for parents who wish to hear their child read. Obviously some of the guidelines are not required. Parents will not need to be concerned with keeping in contact with the rest of the class, and the parent and child will naturally work side by side on easy chairs, rather than using a teacher's desk. At first sight the prior organization to minimize asides would also appear to have less relevance; however, parents should ensure that the sharing of the book takes place when other events in the house are not likely to interfere with the interaction. As Jackson and Hannon (1981) noted, the sharing of a book should not take place with the television on! However, once the arrangements for hearing a child read have been settled then the adult questioning and responses to miscues need not be vastly different whether it is a parent or a teacher who is listening to the child.

1 The teacher needs to position herself so that she can see the complete class.

This first point would appear to be somewhat trivial. However, as this book has been written, in the main, on the basis of a teacher working in the normal classroom setting, with perhaps thirty other children to be provided with adequate learning experiences, then perhaps it is important that the teacher remains aware of other events within that classroom. She is therefore able to react to any event that requires her attention. Furthermore, her observations, albeit from a distance, will enable her to plan for developments that may be required within the room.

2 The teacher and the child should work side by side with the book to be read in front of them.

Working side by side implies a collaborative venture. The teacher and the child have the book in front of them and are working from the same physical level. This is readily achieved by the child standing by the seated teacher at her desk. However, it could also be achieved by the teacher and child sitting on easy chairs in a library corner or by the teacher moving around the room to sit beside a child at his desk or table. Whichever is chosen the most important feature is the togetherness of working side by side.

3 The number of teacher asides should be minimized by the prior organization for the other children in the class.

The first two points imply that the teacher will have organized the classroom so that all the children are aware of the activities and equipment that are available to them. If that organization is successful, the teacher will have the time to concentrate her attention upon the one child reading (or other individual interactions). She will therefore minimize her attention switches during the interaction and consequently be able to demonstrate her involvement with the text and the reader.

4   The interaction should last for about 5 minutes although it is the qualitative aspects of the interaction which are of most importance.

An interaction lasting for approximately 5 minutes would appear to provide an appropriate length for a range of activities to take place. Hearing the child read from the text with the teacher providing sensitive guidance following miscues might be central. However, 5 minutes would also allow for a choice of questioning about the text, relating the text to personal experiences, word recognition, and perhaps some phonic guidance. For older children a longer interaction might be appropriate. Nevertheless the important reminder is that although 5 minutes might provide a reasonable amount of time, it is how that time is used which is crucial. The qualitative aspects of the interaction are more important than the quantitative.

5   The teacher should provide an opening welfare move to reinforce the one-to-one relationship and indicate the empathy of the teacher for the child.

The teacher needs to set the scene for the activity by welcoming the child with words and/or gestures and thus demonstrating the relaxed but purposeful nature of the interaction. Within the 5 minutes of hearing the child read the teacher will be able to demonstrate her empathy for the child by her sensitive response to the reading and her minimal attention switches. However, that empathy can also be demonstrated right from the start of the interaction and the teacher therefore needs to consider her initial comments and actions towards the reader.

6   An optional reference to the previous read or the present read by use of comprehension, word recognition, or phonic questions might be provided.

After the child has been welcomed to the interaction the teacher may wish to move immediately to hearing him read. However, often she will either wish to recall aspects of the text which were previously read or to consider the text to be read on that day. Questions about the illustrations, the text to be read, personal experiences related to the content, specific words, or aspects of phonics are all possibilities at this stage. The aim of the questioning is to help the child prepare and anticipate for the text to be read.

7 **When the child miscues a word the teacher might:**
   (i)   Wait, thus allowing the child time to self-correct.
   (ii) Ignore good errors such as dialect variations and miscues which preserve the essential meaning of the text.
   (iii) Provide a verbal move to assist the child if the miscue is a not so good error.

When the child begins to read, miscues will become evident and it is suggested that as a first strategy the teacher should be prepared to wait and thus give the reader time to reconsider and self-correct. However, if self-correction does not occur the teacher will need to decide whether to intervene or not. If the miscues are dialect variations or preserve the meaning of the text, they might be ignored. Such miscues suggest that the reader is making sense of the text and might therefore be left. However, if the miscue does not retain the meaning, the teacher may need to intervene.

8 **When the child miscues with a not so good error the teacher might:**
   (i)   For miscues at the start of the sentence (in order of preference):
      (a) provide negative feedback as a source of information;
      (b) suggest that the child reads to the end of the sentence in order to gain the context, then try the word again in context;
      (c) provide a suggestion of phonic analysis, thus concentrating on the graphophonic cue system;
      (d) provide the word as a means of maintaining fluency.

(ii) **For miscues within the sentence (in order of preference):**

    (a)   adopt a word cueing move, thus keeping open use of any cue system: graphophonic, syntactic, or semantic;

    (b)   provide negative feedback as a source of information;

    (c)   provide a suggestion of phonic analysis, thus concentrating on the graphophonic cue system;

    (d)   use a comprehension question to assist the child towards the meaning and/or recognition;

    (e)   provide the word as a means of retaining a link with the text.

(iii) The word might be provided more frequently and preferentially for an early beginning reader:

    (a)   to help the reader maintain a link with the text;

    (b)   to demonstrate to the reader the nature of the activity as a shared experience.

If the teacher decides to provide some guidance for miscues which disrupt the meaning, a range of possibilities are available. The possibilities may change according to the position of the miscue in the sentence and also perhaps to the stage of reading development of the child. Nevertheless what the teacher will be trying to do, as she offers verbal moves or perhaps non-verbal gestures, is first to cause minimal disruption to the reader, and second to encourage the reader towards positive problem-solving strategies. The overall aim is to encourage the reader towards eventual effective silent reading.

9   **The teacher might provide positive feedback (preferably in a short form, e.g. 'yes', 'mm', etc.):**

   (i)   **To confirm a child's self-correction.**

   (ii)   **To confirm a child's miscue correction following a teacher verbal move.**

   (iii)   **To praise a correct performance, e.g. sentences or pages (dependent upon progress of the child reading) read correctly.**

   (iv)   **To praise the child upon completion of his read.**

The teacher should not strictly attempt to provide positive feedback at all the points noted above. The list merely indicates the possibilities when information on successful reading and praise can be given. The notion of minimal disruption is again applicable. The aim is to encourage the reader, to inform him of his correct predictions, and to do so in a form that does not distract him from the task of reading.

10 The teacher should provide sufficient directions in order to sustain and develop the interaction.

The teacher may wish to guide and direct the interaction not only with a view to the child's reading development but also, in a normal classroom setting, in order to provide time for activities with other children. That control and direction needs to be provided in a manner which, nevertheless, does not create a barrier to a positive social relationship being established and maintained. Within such a relationship the reader will feel safe to talk about the text and to initiate discussion on various aspects.

11 On completion of the read the teacher might question the child on personal experiences, comprehension, and/or word recognition and phonics as they relate to the text.

When the child completes the book or the passage being read on that day, the teacher may decide to ask questions about that reading. Those questions may relate the text to the reader's personal experiences, be concerned with comprehension, word recognition, or perhaps phonics. Rather than attempting to cover all areas on any one occasion the teacher may instead wish to explore in some depth just one of those aspects.

12 The teacher should provide an appropriate sequence of closing moves which might include both welfare and positive feedback.

Rather than abruptly finishing the interaction the teacher should provide some encouragement and closing remarks in order to conclude the activity in a positive manner. Such conclusions take but the briefest of moments yet importantly can convey so much meaning as to the relationship of the teacher and the reader and of the nature of the activity as a genuine collaborative event.

These guidelines may serve as a starting-point for teachers of young children as they consider, debate, and evaluate the common practice of hearing children read.

Future developments may indicate the way in which these guidelines can be improved. Already in Britain there is a growing interest in the interaction. The work of Elizabeth Goodacre, in particular her booklet (nd) produced by the Centre for the Teaching of Reading, may have provided the stimulus for such interest. More recently Gulliver (1979), Moon (1980), Hale (1980), Hartley (1981), and NATE (1985) have put forward ideas on hearing children read. In addition, of course, the Extending Beginning Reading project (Southgate, Arnold, and Johnson 1981) made comment upon the interaction among first and second year junior school children which included statements by the children about their feelings towards oral reading. A development from that project was the publication by Arnold (1982) in which the diagnostic value of the interaction was emphasized. That text demonstrates how the individual and special needs of the reader might be met within a carefully planned interaction. Other approaches to the child/teacher reading are also available (Waterland 1985) and the involvement of parents in a variety of ways (e.g. Hannon et al. 1985; Topping 1986) indicates the wide interest in this topic. Elsewhere, too, there is an interest in this interaction as a means of developing the child's reading strategies. Clay (1979), Glynn (1980), and McNaughton (1981) in New Zealand have provided insights into hearing children read and some of their ideas have been used in this book. This increasing research together with the important contributions from teachers and children at work in the classroom may well enable the interaction to develop further as a worthwhile teaching activity.

Bibliography

Arnold, H. (1982) *Listening to Chidren Reading*. Sevenoaks: Hodder & Stoughton.

Atkinson, E.J. and Gains, C.W. (1973) *An A to Z of Reading and Subject Books*. Walton on the Hill, Staffs: Nare.

Barrett, T.C. (1968) Taxonomy of the cognitive and affective dimensions of reading comprehension. Unpublished paper, cited in T. Clymer (1968) What is reading? In A. Melnik and J. Merritt (eds) (1972) *Reading: Today and Tomorrow*. London: University of London Press.

Bettelheim, B. and Zelan, K. (1982) *On Learning to Read*. London: Thames & Hudson.

Betts, E.A. (1946) *Foundations of Reading Instruction*. New York: American Book Co.

Biemiller, A. (1970) The development of the use of graphic and contextual information as children learn to read. Reading Research *Quarterly* VI, 1: 75–96.

Bissex, G.L. (1980) *GNYS AT WRK. A Child Learns to Read and Write*. Cambridge, Mass: Harvard University Press.

Boydell, D. (1975) Individual attention – the child's eye view. *Education 3–13* 3, 1: 9–13.

—— (1978) *The Primary Teacher in Action*. London: Open Books.

Burstall, C. (1978) The Matthew effect in the classroom. *Educational Research* 21, 1: 19–25.

Butler, D. and Clay, M.M. (1979) *Reading Begins at Home*. Auckland, NZ: Heinemann Educational.

Campbell, R. (1981) Hearing children read: an infant school example. *Reading* 15, 3: 27–32.

—— (1982) Hearing children read: an exploration and pedagogical analysis of of teacher–child interaction in infant schools. Unpublished M Phil thesis. Open University.

—— (1986) Social relationships in hearing children read. *Reading* 20, 3: 157–67.

Clark, M.M. (1976) *Young Fluent Readers*. London: Heinemann Educational.

Clay, M.M. (1979) *Reading: The Patterning of Complex Behaviour*. London: Heinemann Educational.
Dean, J. (1968) *Reading, Writing and Talking*. London: A & C Black.
—— (1976) Organising language work. In C. Longley (ed.) *Teaching Young Readers*. London: BBC.
DES (1975) *A Language for Life (The Bullock Report)*. London: HMSO.
—— (1978) *Primary Education in England. A Survey by HM Inspectors of Schools*. London: HMSO.
Dolch, E.W. (1961) Individualised reading vs group reading. In J.L. Frost (ed.) *Issues and Innovations in the Teaching of Reading*. Glenview, Ill: Scott, Foresman.
Glynn, T. (1980) Parent–child interaction in remedial reading at home. In M.M. Clark and T. Glynn (eds) (1980) *Reading and Writing for the Child with Difficulties*. Birmingham: Educational.
Goddard, N.L. (1958) *Reading in the Modern Infants' School*. London: University of London Press.
Goodacre, E.J. (nd) *Hearing Children Read*. Reading: Centre for the Teaching of Reading.
—— (1976) Assessment. In C. Longley (ed.) *Teaching Young Readers*. London: BBC.
Goodman, K.S. (1965) A linguistic study of cues and miscues in reading. *Elementary English*, October: 639–43.
——(1967) Reading: a psycholinguistic guessing game. *Journal of the Reading Specialist* 6: 126–35.
—— (1969) Analysis of oral reading miscues: applied linguistics. *Reading Research Quarterly* 1: 9–30.
—— (1973) Psycholinguistic universals in the reading process. In F. Smith (ed.) *Psycholinguistics and Reading*. New York: Holt, Rinehart & Winston.
Goodman, Y.M. (1967) A psycholinguistic description of observed oral reading phenomena in selected young beginning readers. Unpublished Ed D thesis. Wayne State University, Detroit.
—— (1970) Using children's reading miscues for new teaching strategies. *Reading Teacher* 23, 5: 455–9.
Gray, J. (1979) Reading progress in English infant schools: some problems emerging from a study of teacher effectiveness. *British Educational Research Journal* 5, 2: 141–57.
Gulliver, J. (1979) Teachers' assumptions in listening to reading. *Language for Learning* 1: 42–6.
Hale, A. (1980) The social relationships implicit in approaches to reading. *Reading* 14, 2: 24–30.
Hannon, P., Long, R., Weinberger, J., and Whitehurst, L. (1985) *Involving Parents in the Teaching of Reading: Some Key Sources*. Sheffield: USDE Papers in Education.
Harris, A.J. (1979) The effective teacher of reading revisited. *Reading Teacher* 33, 2, November: 135–40.
Hartley, D. (1981) Suggested techniques to employ when hearing a child

read. *Reading* 15, 2: 37–40.

Herber, H.L. (1966) Classroom diagnosis of word study skills. In R. Karlin (ed.) (1973) *Perspectives on Elementary Reading*. New York: Harcourt Brace Jovanovich.

Hewison, J. and Tizard, J. (1980) Parental involvement and reading attainment. *British Journal of Educational Psychology* 50: 209–15.

Hood, J. (1978) Is miscue analysis practical for teachers? *Reading Teacher* 32, 3: 260–6.

Hughes, J.M. (1970) *Aids to Reading*. London: Evans.

—— (1972) *Phonics and the Teaching of Reading*. London: Evans.

—— (1973) *Beginning Reading*. London: Evans.

Ireland, J. (1976) *Word Attack Skills: Teaching 5 to 13 Reading*. London: Macdonald Educational.

Jackson, A. and Hannon, P. (1981) *The Bellfield Reading Project*. Rochdale: Bellfield Community Council, Samson Street, Rochdale OL16 2XW.

King, R. (1978) *All Things Bright and Beautiful? A Sociological Study of Infants' Classrooms*. Chichester: Wiley.

Kohl, H. (1973) *Reading, How to*. Harmondsworth: Penguin.

Kounin, J.S. (1970) *Discipline and Group Management in Classrooms*. Huntington, New York: Robert E. Kreiger.

Mackay, D., Thompson, B., and Schaub, P. (1970) *Breakthrough to Literacy – Teachers' Manual*. London: Longman.

McNaughton, S. (1981) The influence of immediate teacher correction on self-corrections and proficient oral reading. *Journal of Reading Behaviour* XIII, 4: 367–71.

Marchbanks, G. and Levin, H. (1965) Cues by which children recognise words. *Journal of Educational Psychology* 56, 2: 57–61.

Meek, M. (1982) *Learning to Read*. London: Bodley Head.

Moon, C. (1973) *Individualized Reading*. Reading: Centre for the Teaching of Reading.

—— (1980) Don't interrupt! *Child Education* March: 25.

Morris, J.M. (1966) *Standards and Progress in Reading*. Slough: NFER.

—— (1974) *Language in Action-Resource Book*. London: Macmillan.

Moyle, D. (1968) *The Teaching of Reading*. London: Ward Lock Educational.

Natchez, G. (1975) *Gideon – a Boy who Hates Learning in School*. New York: Basic Books.

NATE (1985) *Children Reading to their Teachers*. Sheffield: NATE.

Pehrsson, R.S.V. (1974) The effects of teacher interference during the process of reading, or how much of a helper is Mr Gelper. *Journal of Reading* May: 617–21.

Potts, J. (1976) *Beyond Initial Reading*. London: Allen & Unwin.

Resnick, L.B. (1972) Teacher behaviour in the informal classroom. *Journal of Curriculum Studies* 4: 99–109.

Roberts, G.R. (1973) *Early Stages in Reading*. Unit 6, PE261, Reading Development Course, Bletchley: Open University Press.

Schonell, F.J. (1951) *The Phycology and Teaching of Reading*.
   Edinburgh: Oliver & Boyd.
Sinclair, J.McH. and Coulthard, R.M. (1975) *Towards an Analysis of
   Discourse*. Oxford: Oxford University Press.
Skinner, B.F. (1968) *The Technology of Teaching*. New York: Appleton-
   Century-Crofts.
Smith, F. (1971) *Understanding Reading*. New York: Holt, Rinehart, &
   Winston.
—— (1978) *Reading*. Cambridge: Cambridge University Press.
Smith, F. and Goodman, K.S. (1971) On the psycholinguistic method of
   teaching reading. In F. Smith (ed.) (1973) *Psycholinguistics and
   Reading*. New York: Holt, Rinehart, & Winston.
Southgate, V. (1968) Formulae for beginning reading tuition. *Educational
   Research* II, 1: 23–30.
Southgate, V., Arnold, H., and Johnson, S. (1981) *Extending Beginning
   Reading*. London: Heinemann Educational.
Thackray, D. (1980) Criteria for a reading scheme. In G. Bray and A.K.
   Pugh (eds) *The Reading Connection*. London: Ward Lock Educational.
—— (1981) The text and the reading scheme In L.J. Chapman (ed.) *The
   Reader and the Text*. London: Heinemann Educational.
Topping, K. (1986) W.H.I.C.H. parental involvement in reading scheme?
   A guide for practitioners. *Reading* 20, 3: 148–56.
Tough, J. (1979) *Talk for Teaching and Learning*. London: Ward Lock
   Educational.
Veatch, J. (1978) *Reading in the Elementary School*. New York: Wiley.
Vincent, D. and Cresswell, M. (1976) *Reading Tests in the Classroom*.
   Slough: NFER.
Waterland, L. (1985) *Read with Me*. Stroud: Thimble Press.
Weber, R.M. (1970) A linguistic analysis of first-grade reading errors.
   Reading Research Quarterly 3, 427–52.
West Sussex County Council (1976) *Children and Language*.
   Basingstoke: Globe Education.

Name Index

Subject Index